Praise for
The Art of Vinemaking

"With *The Art of Vinemaking*, Bette Dickinson has offered her readers a deeply moving invitation to be formed into the people God longs for us to become. And like the vine dressing she describes, this book is to be ingested, digested and metabolized slowly. For indeed, you will not want to miss a morsel or moment of the beauty and goodness that you will find herein. But do not fear to tread slowly over the words on these pages. For in honoring the pace our author sets, we will find ourselves becoming more than we could imagine."

Curt Thompson, MD
Author of *The Soul of Desire* and
The Deepest Place

"In *The Art of Vinemaking*, author Bette Dickinson both diagnoses the malady infecting our culture and offers a sure cure. Dickinson invites us to resist the urge to be always busy, accomplishing more, and producing faster, and instead to slow down, to experience God's love, and to connect with ourselves and the world around us. Based on Scripture and scientific data and steeped in beautiful imagery and poignant metaphors, *The Art of Vinemaking* is a welcome departure from the productivity-focused society we find ourselves in. If you are like me, you need this book!"

Dave Ferguson
Author of *B.L.E.S.S.* and *Hero Maker*

"For decades, the vine and branches in John 15 have been the heartbeat of our lives and ministry. Abiding in Jesus is the central invitation to us all. In her book, *The Art of Vinemaking*, Bette Dickinson offers a beautiful and masterful guide into the rhythms and seasons of the vine, drawing us ultimately to Jesus himself who modeled the pattern of life, death, and resurrection. This book is a must-read for all who care deeply about their own formation, and that of their faith community."

Gem & Alan Fadling
Founders of Unhurried Living
Authors of *What Does Your Soul Love?*

"In her latest book, *The Art of Vinemaking*, Bette Dickinson masterfully reveals to us the hidden world of vinedressing in order to help us see the roots of a truly Jesus-shaped spirituality. All at once she exposes the futility of a productivity-driven life and identity, she awakens an appetite for abundance and flourishing, and she guides readers in cultivating the kind of spiritual fruit that bears wholeheartedness and vitality. *The Art of Vinemaking* is a feast of words and images which are as urgently needed as they are beautiful and true."

Michael John Cusick
Author of *Sacred Attachment* & Founder,
Restoring the Soul

"In *The Art of Vinemaking*, Bette Dickinson writes from the grounded perspective of one who has walked among the vines—literally. Her conversations with a local vinedresser and her question, 'What does a vinedresser pay attention to when tending vines?' opened a journey of discovery unlike anything I've encountered in teachings on John 15:1–11. Drawing deeply from her own life and experiences, Dickinson offers a rare blend of insight and invitation. This book is a true gift, calling readers to walk Creator's Good Road through the vineyard of life. Highly recommended."

Terry M. Wildman
Lead Translator and Project Manager,
First Nations Version: New Testament and
Psalms and Proverbs

The Art of Vinemaking

Spiritual Flourishing in a Productivity-Driven Culture

BY BETTE DICKINSON

B⬤UNDLESS
PUBLISHING

BOUNDLESS
PUBLISHING

Boundless Publishing
PO Box 14006, Abbotsford BC, V2T 0B4
https://www.boundlessenterprise.org/

Co-publisher:
The People's Seminary Press
Burlington, WA 98233
www.peoplesseminary.org

Boundless Publishing is the publishing division of Boundless Enterprise.

All Scripture quotations, unless otherwise indicated, are taken from The Holy Bible, New International Version ®, NIV ®. Copyright © 1973, 1978, 1984, 2011 by Biblica, Inc™. Used by permission of Zondervan. All rights reserved worldwide. The "NIV" and "New International Version" are trademarks registered in the United States Patent and Trademark Office by Biblica, Inc™.

Stories in this book have been used with permission.

Cover image and interior images are by Bette Dickinson. All rights reserved.

The publisher cannot verify the accuracy or functionality of website URLs used in this book beyond the date of publication.

Cover Design: Jude May, https://www.judemaydesign.com/
Interior Design: Vicki Frye

ISBN: 979-8-218-74375-8

Author: Bette Dickinson

For Lauren,

who modeled a life of abiding

in the True Vine.

— ———————— • O • ———————— —

"I am the true vine, and my Father is the gardener.
He cuts off every branch in me that bears no fruit,
while every branch that does bear fruit he prunes
so that it will be even more fruitful.
You are already clean because of
the word I have spoken to you.
Remain in me, as I also remain in you.
No branch can bear fruit by itself;
it must remain in the vine.
Neither can you bear fruit
unless you remain in me.

I am the vine; you are the branches.
If you remain in me and I in you,
you will bear much fruit;
apart from me you can do nothing.
If you do not remain in me,
you are like a branch that is
thrown away and withers;
Such branches are picked up,
thrown into the fire and burned.
If you remain in me and my words remain in you,
ask whatever you wish, and it will be done for you.
This is to my Father's glory, that you bear much fruit,
showing yourselves to be my disciples."

John 15:1–8

— ———————— • O • ———————— —

Contents

Foreword

by Danielle Strickland

I don't think most of us fully realize what shapes our beliefs and behaviors. Years ago, I spoke with a Rwandan pastor who had taken a Mindset Training program through World Relief. I had heard devastating reports of domestic abuse in his region; yet, within a single year of introducing this training, those rates had fallen drastically. I needed to understand how.

He explained it like this: *"It's like a tree."* The fruit—especially the bad fruit—must be acknowledged, not ignored or hidden. But the fruit isn't the root problem. The branches are the behaviors from which the fruit hangs, and even these are not the deepest issue. The trunk represents the values that feed those behaviors.

Still, deeper yet, beneath the surface, buried in the soil, lies the rooted belief system. It is from these unseen roots that values grow, behaviors emerge, and fruit appears. If you want to transform the fruit, you must unearth and heal the roots.

I've never forgotten this.

We live in a culture obsessed with behavior modification, convinced that doing more, better, faster is how change happens. The self-help industry thrives on this illusion, yet it fails us. Rarely do we pause long enough—or know how to pause—to trace the fruit of our lives back to the belief systems buried beneath.

I was reminded of this during one of our Infinitum prayer days—a community practice where we offer our most precious resource—time—to God. We begin with guided prayer together, then step into solitude with curated prompts. It has become essential to my formation.

On one occasion, Bette, our wise and steady leader, interviewed a vineyard keeper, Dave Bos. As they spoke about tending vineyards—and how this differs from industrial farming—something stirred in me. Two things happened at once: my mind expanded and my heart was pierced. This is what the Scriptures call *metanoia*: a deep turning, a repentance that transforms.

As I listened, I saw the links between the unhealthy fruit in my life and the behaviors that bore them. I traced them further, to the values beneath, and finally, to the belief systems I hadn't realized I carried. That Rwandan teaching was coming alive in me again. I began to see how the very framework of my Christian life—my measurements, expectations, and desires—had been shaped by an industrial mindset.

Let me explain:

I've measured my worth by productivity. I tell myself otherwise, but deep down, I am driven by an insatiable hunger to do more. This hunger springs from a belief system rooted in protecting my image, earning my identity, and finding my value in performance. It's steeped in a capitalistic mindset that looks at land—and people—and asks, *What can I get?* rather than *What can I give?*

My outcomes have been measured by size, speed, and numbers, not by health, longevity, or fruitfulness. I've prized short-term gains over long-term goodness. Like industrial farming, this mindset is exploitative, utilitarian, self-centered, and ultimately destructive. Land—and people—are used up and discarded, left to bear the waste of what was taken.

And while I've often railed against these injustices in society, I'm beginning to see how that same spirit has quietly possessed me, too.

As a leader, I've encouraged people to give more to ministry, sometimes at the expense of their families, bodies, and lives. I've participated in "working" people for the benefit of "the work"—and for that, I am genuinely sorry. I see now how my own pursuit of success was often disconnected from the health of the wider ecosystem of God's kingdom, inattentive to the needs of local communities, and too focused on my patch of soil.

This is just the beginning of the long unravelling of toxic attitudes, the excavation of hidden beliefs. Billie Holiday sang of *strange fruit*—lynched bodies hanging from trees—a chilling metaphor for what people justify when driven by corrupted, unseen roots.

This may sound like bad news, but it isn't. This is the good work of repentance, of exposing the roots to the light. True repentance brings sorrow, but leaves no regrets.

The Transformation

This is what this book begins to do. It names what must be uprooted and plants what must grow. As I listened to the voices behind these pages, I was struck by the wisdom of a true vineyard keeper—one who, when the vine fails to bear fruit, doesn't discard it, but tends the soil, examines the interdependent web of relationships, and nurtures the ecosystem until the vine can flourish again.

The words and experience Bette offers remind me of God—the master winemaker—who does not merely demand results or walk away when we feel spent, but who longs for our healing, our wholeness, and our rootedness within the living, breathing ecosystem of the kingdom. The invitation is to "remain in him" because he is the maker, the keeper, and the vineyard owner who knows what we need.

May you find the slow, deep, and beautiful fruitful process of cultivating a life connected to the source of all. May you, too, have a metanoia experience that awakens your mind and moves your heart towards Life in all its fullness. May you unravel the work of the world "domination system" that has malformed you in its image, and may you be re-formed and transformed by the renewing of your mind through true submission to the ways of Jesus.

I'll meet you at the table where, with Jesus, we will drink New Wine together and remind ourselves of the patient and thorough work of the One who pours us an overflowing cup that quenches the deepest thirst within us all.

Until then, may you be rooted in the soil of God's Love so that together we might just grasp how wide, how deep, how long, and how high this Love truly is.

Introduction

I had arrived early at a vineyard and winery on Old Mission Peninsula in Traverse City, Michigan. I wanted a few quiet moments to walk among the vines alone. The October sky was thick with clouds, and the crisp air rolled in from the bay, carrying the scent of decaying leaves.

If Romans 1:20 is true, that God's invisible qualities are revealed through what he has made, then surely there was something these vines had to tell me about God and perhaps, about myself, too.

I wandered slowly, partly to pay close attention, partly because I was exhausted from the preparations I had been making for a ministry conference I was directing the next day. I felt a quiet kinship with these weary vines at the end of harvest that were sagging under the weight of heavy, ripened fruit. Their once vibrant green leaves had faded to mustard yellow with deep burgundy spots creeping inward from the tips.

I crouched beside one of the vines, adjusting my camera lens to frame the woody, grayish-brown trunk nestled beneath the canopy of leaves and fruit. The gnarled base, thick and knotted, bore the marks of years of pruning, with remnants of severed branches jutting out sideways in remembrance of past seasons. As the trunk rose toward the trellis, it tapered upward, bending in generous curves, its arms outstretched as if lifted in quiet praise.

And yet, for all my careful study of the deep lines and curves of each vine, the truth embedded in them felt out of reach. It felt more like trying to decipher an ancient language, its secrets lingering just beyond my grasp. I needed a guide. Someone who had gleaned from creation's wisdom and could interpret her language to me.

I needed someone like Dave.

Dave was a vinedresser and winemaker who had recently moved to Traverse City, Michigan, from Napa Valley to consult for vineyard owners on organic farming. He and his wife, Jackie, were dreaming of one day starting a wine garden and label in the area.

When I called to set up our meeting, I told Dave I wanted to take pictures of the vines to use as source images for a painting I was working on. But beneath that request was a deeper longing. Like many followers of Jesus, the words in John 15:1, "I am the true vine, and my Father is the vinedresser" (ESV) had deeply shaped my spiritual life. Now, I had the chance to meet a real vinedresser using cultivation practices akin to those in Jesus' day. I was full of anticipation ... and questions.

What does a vinedresser actually do?

What did Jesus' audience, rooted in an agrarian society, naturally understand about vines that I didn't?

And, perhaps the most pressing question: how do vinedressers help a vine become "abundantly fruitful" in the way Jesus described?

When Dave pulled into the parking lot, his gracious presence greeted me with joy and enthusiasm. Dressed in a black hooded sweatshirt, jeans, and a Detroit baseball cap, he invited me to hop into his navy pickup truck to visit a nearby vineyard he had been tending just down the road.

When we pulled onto the dirt road of the vineyard, rows of vines blanketed the hills in every direction. Dave led me on a walking tour through the vineyard like an artist eager to show me his craft. He explained each part of the vine, from the leaves and lateral branches to the cane laid along the trellis. It was clear that *vinedressing* was his thing, and he was thrilled to host an eager participant like me.

As we studied some Merlot vines flush with fruit, I asked, "So, what do vinedressers pay attention to when tending vines?"

What Dave shared with me next began to totally reshape the way I view the spiritual life: "Vinedressers don't pay much attention to the fruit."

I blinked. "Wait—what!?"

This was in direct opposition to everything I had been taught.

"It's not that they don't care about the fruit," he continued, "It's just that, by that point, their work is already done. All that matters to good vinedressers is the health, quality, and vitality of their vines. If they pay attention to those things, good fruit will be the natural byproduct."

Oh.

There was something about this statement that caught me totally off guard. And yet, something about his words resonated deeply. They illuminated a truth I had long sensed but couldn't articulate.

> *The vinedresser's primary concern*
> *isn't fruit—it's flourishing.*

I found myself sinking into a holy hush as I took in this wisdom that seemed so obvious to Dave, yet so far out of reach from my context. Because the reality was, I was living in a world that, unlike Dave, paid *a lot* of attention to the fruit.

All of a sudden, I was back in a Panera Bread booth in 2014. I was a campus staff member in a college ministry, sitting across from my supervisor for my annual performance review. As he slid our annual field report across the table, my heart rate ticked up. I knew what was coming. On this sheet were our numbers for the year: the number of students involved in our ministry, the number of small groups, and the number of conversions. And—it had been a particularly difficult year.

After several years of steady growth, student leaders started dropping like flies due to depression, burnout, or overcommitment, and the ministry began to shrink.

Then came a series of traumatic events.

Just weeks before that review, one of our student leaders had a moral failure, my co-worker's wife left him, and I suffered a miscarriage—all in the same week. But, the conversation during my performance review focused on why the numbers were so low and what we could do better next year.

As someone who tends to measure her worth by her achievements, I had spent the entire year pushing myself to meet expectations, striving to hit our goals. But, when the numbers on that sheet of paper fell far below what we had hoped for, I felt like a failure. There had been little discussion about the pain from the trauma that year and how it impacted our wellbeing as leaders—or the ministry itself.

Five years later, standing in the vineyard, the dissonance between performance metrics and the health of our leaders resurfaced. Dave's words challenged everything I had been conditioned to believe about fruitfulness.

The Productivity-Driven Approach to Fruit

In Western culture, especially since the Industrial Revolution, we tend to have an obsession with measurable outcomes. So, when we hear the word "fruitful," we typically think of large-scale production. Whether it is in a ministry context or in the marketplace, there is a sense that it is *always* "harvest season." We always need something to show for our efforts; something to reap. And each year's harvest needs to be greater than the last. The questions are always the same:

> "How much fruit was produced?"
>
> "What is the value of the harvest?"
>
> "How efficient is the harvesting process?"

But those weren't the questions Dave was asking.

And I began to wonder: were these the questions God was asking?

It's not that the fruit is irrelevant. Farmers like Dave care deeply about the harvest and the wine it produces. And, like Jesus said, when we bear "much fruit," it brings glory to the Father.[1] But, our understanding of what "much fruit" looks like and how it's cultivated has often been shaped more by a productivity-driven culture than by the values of the Father Vinedresser.

Productivity itself isn't inherently wrong. But, when we primarily strive for tangible metrics of success like numerical growth, attendance, or revenue, we risk neglecting the intangible fruits God cares about most: relational depth, character formation, and the wholeness of creation and communities.

> We might celebrate the growth of a megachurch,
> only to grieve later the moral failure of one of its pastors.

---

1. John 15:8.

We might applaud a soaring profit margin,
only to discover it was built on the backs of exploited
workers or child labor.

We might praise a songwriter who climbs the charts,
only to watch their life unravel under the crushing
pressure of performance.

A productivity-driven culture rewards measurable success with financial gain, increased influence, and upward mobility. These rewards aren't inherently evil, but when they drive us, we tend to push ourselves, others, and creation toward demands that are ultimately dehumanizing. Our relationships become transactional at best, and exploitative at worst. Our character withers, showing up in rotten fruit. We begin to value people based on what they contribute to the bottom line—elevating the wealthy, influential, and powerful, while overlooking the poor, the marginalized, and the oppressed.

Activists call this system *empire*.

Psychologists call it *narcissism*.

Theologians call it *the rulers, authorities, and powers of this dark world*.[2]

For our purposes, we'll call it: *the Productivity-Driven Approach*.

---

2. Ephesians 6:12.

The Fallout of a Productivity-Driven Approach

Standing in the vineyard with Dave that day, I realized just how much I'd internalized this way of life. Over the years, I've watched friends and family burn out beneath the weight of *the Productivity-Driven Approach.*

I thought of the student leaders I had shepherded, and the times I overlooked the weariness in their eyes, pushing them to invite their friends to conferences and events, unintentionally reinforcing a performance-driven mindset.

I thought about the students we led to faith, but wondered if we had helped them connect deeply enough to Jesus so they could withstand life's storms.

I thought of relationships that remained surface-level because they revolved around projects and goals rather than love and belonging.

I thought of many young leaders who left ministry after just a few short years because their souls couldn't bear the pressure and pace.

But, this wasn't just a ministry problem—it was, and is, *everywhere.* We live in a culture that constantly demands more: more results, more accomplishments, more milestones.

In business, employees are crushed under performance metrics and quarterly reviews.

In healthcare, long hours and quotas leave little room for quality, compassionate care.

In education, teachers are forced to "teach to the test," while students struggle under a system that values achievement over true learning.

Creation itself groans under this way of life. The soil, depleted from overproduction, suffers from the constant extraction of resources without rest or replenishment. The land is as exhausted as we are.

The question remains: *Is this the kind of fruit the Father seeks?*

Maybe, like me, you feel this in your bones—a sense that something has been diminishing in health, quality, and vitality within you and your community.

Perhaps you feel the dissonance between western culture's obsession with measurable outcomes and the resulting experience of depletion, disconnection, and spiritual malnourishment.

Maybe, like me, you feel like the world has run out of wine.

Running Out of Wine

You may recall the story in John 2, when Jesus turned water into wine for a wedding feast. When the wine runs out, Mary simply turns to Jesus and says, "They have no more wine," then tells the servants, "Do whatever he tells you."

Quietly, behind the scenes, Jesus spares the couple the shame of this moment by partnering with the servants to transform six stone jars used for Jewish ceremonial washing into an abundance of fine wine. When the master of the banquet tastes it, he exclaims, "You have saved the best till now."[3]

There is much more going on here than a wedding celebration at risk of being ruined by a lack of alcohol.

Throughout Scripture, wine is a symbol of something much deeper.

In the Jewish imagination, the vine represented the people of Israel. God, the Vinedresser, planted his people in the Promised Land[4] and tended them with care. Wine was the fruit of this covenant; the overflow of intimate communion between God, the Bridegroom, and his people, the Bride.

Wine, especially at a wedding, was a foretaste of this covenant fulfillment. It was a picture of right-relationship with God, where God's presence, justice, and blessing flowed into the world like the finest wine, bringing joy, abundance, and flourishing for all.

Yet, the prophets lamented that Israel did not live into this vision. Justice was perverted. The covenant was abandoned. The vine God planted yielded only sour grapes.[5]

So, when the wine runs out at the wedding in Cana, it's not just a logistical problem. It's a prophetic symbol. At the very place where a covenant of love was meant to overflow with joy, there is an emptiness.

And it's precisely at this point of emptiness that Jesus begins his public ministry.

---

3. John 2:10.

4. Psalm 80:8.

5. Isaiah 5:2b.

In a world that had run out of wine, Jesus came to bring the good stuff. The stone jars, once used for Jewish purification rituals to uphold the old covenant, are now filled with something entirely new.

This moment in John 2 signals the arrival of a new kind of marriage covenant; a loving union that yields an enduring wine.

In John 15, Jesus shows us what this covenant looks like. Declaring himself the "true vine," he announces that he has come to fulfill and embody Israel's calling. Where Israel, God's chosen vine, failed to bear lasting fruit, Jesus prevails. His life overflowed with the fruit of righteousness and justice the Father longed for. And through his self-giving love, he opens a way for us to be grafted into his life.

No longer do we need to strive to uphold the covenant through ritual in order to stay connected to God. Instead, we are invited into a living communion with Christ. As branches joined to the True Vine, his life flows through us—ripening quality fruit that will be harvested, pressed, and poured out like a fine wine for the sake of the world.

Like ancient Israel, our modern world feels like a wedding feast where the wine has run dry. We have been trying to squeeze out fruit for the kingdom through our productivity and performance. Many of us have reached the end of ourselves. We are spiritually, relationally, and emotionally depleted, longing for quality connection, meaning, depth, and joy.

I wonder, if Mary were to step into our homes or churches today, would she look around with a mixture of empathy and conviction and say, "They have no more wine"?

If the story at Cana shows us anything, it's this: when the wine runs out, Jesus doesn't refill the empty cups with the same cheap wine.

He brings transformation; the kind that yields the finest wine in abundance.

The kind that flows from his love and presence within us.

The kind that tastes like joy and laughter erupting at a wedding celebration.

As I've listened to Dave describe his slow, attentive approach to vinedressing, I've begun to get a taste of this kind of wine. I'm starting to see fruitfulness in a new light—not as something we hustle to produce, but as something that ripens over time through loving cultivation and intimate union with the Vine.

I've come to call this way of life *The Art of Vinemaking*.

It's an art, because it embraces the slow, creative, and relational process our Vinedresser undertakes as he shapes us, the branches. Like all true art, it is organic and mysterious, and it unfolds in the sacred space between the temporal and the eternal. And it is *vinemaking* because, like the intentional craft of winemaking, God carefully cultivates us, the branches, through every season—so that we bear fruit that is an expression of his kingdom.

This isn't just a metaphor for growth. It is an invitation into a way of life.

An Invitation into the Art of Vinemaking

That day in the vineyard, Dave graciously and enthusiastically answered my questions, but he offered me so much more than this. He invited me to learn not just from his technique, but from the culture he creates in the vineyard—rooted in love and relationship, and so different from our own.

Over the last six years, I've become something of a vinedresser's apprentice. I've spent hours in the vineyard with my camera in hand, capturing the beauty of the vine and discovering God's wisdom woven into creation.

What I have learned from the vines has liberated me from the relentless pace of a productivity-driven life. I've discovered a rhythm of abiding in Jesus that releases striving, ripens fruit from this deeply rooted place, and expresses my truest self.

And that's why I wrote this book—in hopes that together, we might embrace a new way of fruitfulness.

With Dave as our guide, we'll walk through the vineyards together, exploring the rich beauty of this approach. We'll get close enough to breathe in the vine's blossoms, hear the snap of dormant branches, and encounter the deep transformation that unfolds when we surrender to the sacred rhythms of the vine.

In **Part I**, we'll lay the foundation for *The Art of Vinemaking* by introducing the core elements of this story: the characters, the setting, and the plot.

- **In Chapter 1**, we meet *the Vinedresser*, the one who shapes the culture of the vineyard. We'll contrast *the Productivity-Driven Approach* with what I call a *Flourishing Approach*, and begin to glimpse the Father's manner of tending us.

- **In Chapter 2**, we'll turn to the setting. Just as the environment of a story shapes its characters, the place where a vine grows profoundly affects the fruit it bears; what the wine world calls **terroir**. We'll reflect on how our Vinedresser plants each of us within a particular context and draws out the unique gifts of that place through the fruit we yield.

- ❧ **In Chapter 3**, we'll meet *the Vine and Branches*. Here, we'll explore what it truly means to abide in Christ, the True Vine, through the lens of relational attachment. We'll discover how fruitfulness flows not from striving, but from union with Christ.

- ❧ **In Chapter 4**, we'll begin to trace the plot—the cyclical rhythm of Christ's death, resurrection, and life. This rhythm, illustrated in the graphic below, becomes the structure for the rest of the book.

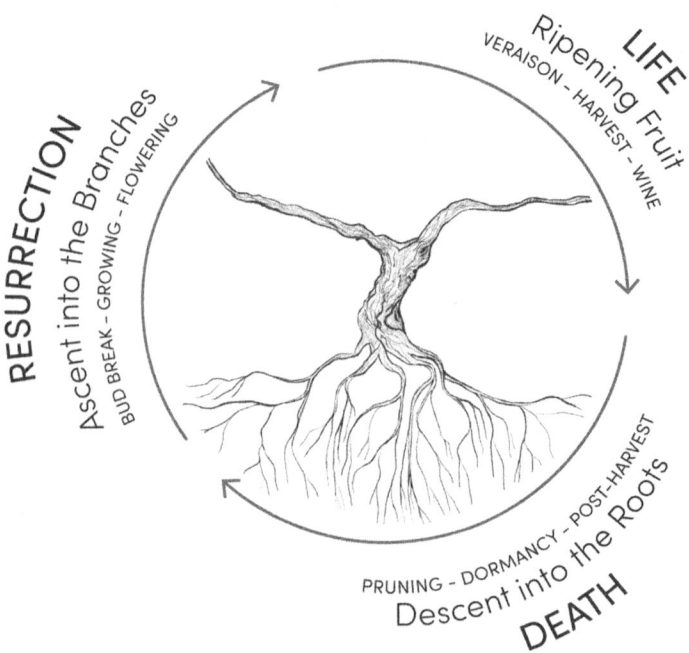

In **Parts II, III, and IV**, we'll discover what it looks like to abide in Christ's death, resurrection, and life, uncovering the unique gifts of each season of the vine.

In **Part II**, we explore what it means to *die with Christ*, as his energy descends into the roots. From post-harvest to pruning, we'll recover our *belovedness* in seasons of loss and surrender.

In **Part III**, we consider what it means to *rise with Christ*, as his energy ascends into the branches. From bud break to flowering, we'll discover our *belonging* within the community of branches.

In **Part IV**, we reflect on what it means to *bear the fruit of Christ's life*, as his energy channels into the fruit. From ripening to the pouring of wine, we'll contemplate the kind of quality fruit that emerges from a deeply rooted life, offered as a *blessing* for the world.

In each season, we'll learn how to surrender to the Vinedresser's loving cultivation, the kind that leads to thriving and bears lasting, eternal fruit. Throughout this book, you'll encounter vineyard terms and practices drawn from both Scripture and the art of winemaking. If any words are unfamiliar, you'll find a helpful glossary of key terms at the back of the book. Feel free to flip there as you read.

As I've worked on this book, I've come to see my role more clearly—like the servants at the wedding in Cana. They didn't create the miracle, Jesus did. But they participated in it by filling jars with water, quietly and faithfully behind the scenes. And that's what the creative process has been like.

Over these past six years, as I've abided in loving union with Jesus, the True Vine, I've been gathering his living water and inspiration from the vineyard into the "jars" of my words, art, and prayers—in the studio and on the page.

My hope is that as I pour this book out in love for you, he might turn it into new wine: something beautiful, something sacred, something that carries the flavor of the kingdom when you taste it.

With every stroke and word, I long to create a safe and sacred space for you to encounter the boundless love of the Vinedresser and to empower you to live into your unique identity as a branch of the True Vine. As I share my story, I pray you'll hear God's invitation for your own—and that you'll discover how to ripen the fruit of the kingdom in your own terroir.

May this book feel like a table set with an abundant feast, and may each chapter pour you a glass of wine that carries the story of the Vine in every sip.

Part I:
The Story of the Vine

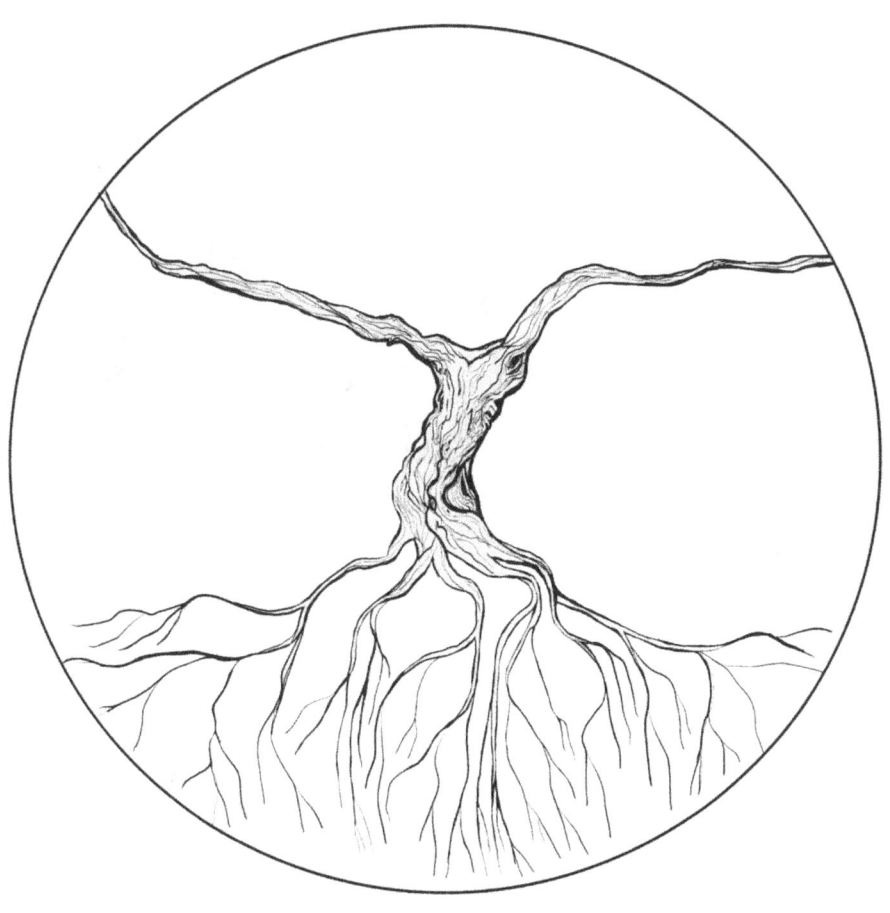

Chapter 1:

The Vinedresser

"I am the true vine, and my Father is the vinedresser."
John 15:1 (ESV)

On a cloudless morning in July, I stand in a vineyard in Elk Rapids with Dave. He draws my attention to one particular vine that has no fruit. It is lively and green, but barren.

Dave explains, "I took the fruit off this year because the vine just wasn't healthy enough to bear it."

As he says this, my heart sinks. I feel in my body the times in my life when I wasn't healthy enough to ripen visible fruit. I feel this for the church in the West in its rapid season of decline. I feel it for the many dear ones I love who are going through trauma or loss, who need several seasons to slow down, grieve, and heal before any signs of fruit begin to emerge.

But then what Dave shares next, as he gestures to this vine, gives me so much hope. "I'm not mad at this vine for not being healthy enough to bear fruit. I'm going to do everything within my power to cultivate it back to health."

My throat catches for a moment. "Everything within my power to cultivate it back to health?"

What if the very places we feel ashamed for being unable to "produce," because of unhealth, God looks upon us with this same kind of merciful compassion that says, "I see you there struggling, and instead of letting you bear fruit that will burn you out I'm removing it for now—so you can heal."

Can you surrender to the care of *this* kind of Vinedresser? One who sometimes removes the fruit for the sake of your health?

What is the Vinedresser Like?

When Jesus said the words, *"I am the true vine, and my Father is the vinedresser,"* I wonder what kind of vinedresser the disciples had in mind.

A.W. Tozer famously wrote, "What comes into our minds when we think about God is the most important thing about us."[2] So, when you hear the word vinedresser, what do you see?

Do you imagine a boss putting the squeeze on you to yield buckets of fruit?

---

1. John 15:1, ESV.

2. A. W. Tozer, *The Knowledge of the Holy* (New York: Harper & Brothers, 1961), 1.

Or someone like Dave who says of his vines, *"I am going to do everything in my power to help you thrive"?*

What is God's approach to cultivating us?

Two Different Approaches to Cultivation

The word *cultivation* shares its root with *culture*—the values, practices, and behaviors that shape a community. In a vineyard, it's the vinedresser who sets the tone for this culture. And one of the clearest ways they do this is by what they choose to measure. Because what we measure reveals what we value.

For Dave, an organic vinedresser, measurement is not about spreadsheets or quotas; it's deeply embodied and relational. He runs the leaves between his fingers, feeling for subtle signs: rubbery means well-watered, papery suggests thirst. He studies the canopy's color and shape, reading the story told by tendrils—their presence signaling growth, their absence hinting at stress.

He notices the diversity of life in the ecosystem—cover crops, insects, birds, microorganisms—because the more diverse, the healthier the vineyard. And when fruit begins to ripen, his "metrics" are as personal as tasting berries for the delicate balance of sugar and acidity. His measurements focus on the signs of life, not the pace or scale of production.

But many of us have been shaped by a very different set of values. We live in a culture that measures people like machines—by output, speed, and efficiency. In a world driven by performance metrics and profit margins, where CEOs and political leaders often prioritize accumulation over care, it's worth asking how deeply these models have shaped our view of God.

Contemplation Over Exploitation

In *The Life We're Looking For*, Andy Crouch quotes the late Leanne Payne, who once said, "We either contemplate or we exploit." He explains:

> *"Exploitation asks, 'What can this person—or thing, for that matter—do for me?' Contemplation asks, 'Who or what am I beholding, without regard for their usefulness to me?'"*[3]

This same contrast shows up in the vineyard. The vinedressers who cultivate from a *Flourishing Approach* lead with observation. One could even say good vinedressers contemplate their vines as they get close to notice, listen, and feel each vine.

Dave walks the rows with compassionate curiosity, getting into the vineyards frequently to behold them with a sense of wonder and attunement to their needs. He responds with small, almost imperceivable changes to help them grow. "It's these small changes over time," Dave tells me, "that create the 'it' factor in wine."

But not all vinedressers take this approach. My friend Susie Lipps—founder of Conversations in the Vineyard—described what happens when Industrialized Vineyards adopt a *Productivity-Driven Approach*:

---

3. Andy Crouch, *The Life We're Looking For: Reclaiming Relationship in a Technological World* (New York: Penguin Press, 2022), 32–33.

There is no "contemplation" of each vine, only machines that drive along each row to till the soil, trim the vines, and harvest the fruit. They are not interested in great wine, just lots of it.

Pruning is not done with great care and understanding of each vine, but hurriedly, in service of the time clock. Many of these vineyards only live for 10–15 years before becoming diseased or exhausted. They are pulled out and the ground is not left long enough to recover before a new vineyard is planted. Considering that it takes almost three years to get fruit, it's basically a "churn and burn" approach.[4]

But God is not a vinedresser like this.

He is not sitting on his throne fretting about the yields we produce.

He doesn't have a profit margin that he needs to make every year.

He doesn't take a "churn and burn" approach that produces barrels of cheap wine from our lives.

He isn't interested in making something lucrative out of us.

He is after something far more compelling—he is interested in making us whole. He is interested in making us like him. And as such, he takes the long view, patiently nurturing us to bring forth our very best.

God beholds his creation without regard for its usefulness to him. As his image-bearers, we reflect him when we choose contemplation over exploitation—when we see others not as means to an end, but as sacred masterpieces of God.

---

4. Susie Lipps, personal correspondence, used with permission.

It's beholding the woman at the checkout counter at the grocery store, looking her in the eyes, and seeing her as a beloved daughter, instead of merely a means to purchase our food.

It's contemplating the beauty of our team members as we work on a project, standing in silent awe of the wild mystery of their gifts, unique facial expressions, and quirks, beyond what we need from them to complete the project.

It's taking a moment to study our spouse's face at the dinner table, delighting in the wrinkles along the edges of their eyes and the years of laughter that put them there, more than how we would like them to do the dishes after the meal.

When we live this way, everything shifts. We begin to ripen the rich fruit of the kingdom.

The most beautiful things in this world take time to grow—and your formation is no exception. God is cultivating you to bear fruit with eternal value—fruit that reflects his beauty and glory to the world. And this kind of fruit can only grow through slow, intentional, loving care.

A Foundation of Love

Of all the plants Jesus could have chosen to describe our relationship with him, he chose the vine; one of the most high-maintenance plants around. Unlike trees that need little attention, a vine demands constant care. What does this tell us about God?

It tells us that he wants to be an *active* participant in your life and formation. He leans in. He gets close. He visits often. Why? Because he loves you.

Vinedressing is slow, hard work that yields meager results in the short term. But good vinedressers don't do it for the money. They do it because they *love* vines.

When I watch Dave in the vineyard, I never get a sense that he is in a hurry or trying to speed up the growth process. He isn't anxious about the harvest—when it will arrive and how much it will yield. Instead, I get the sense of his complete and utter delight in simply being there in the vineyard with these vines and watching them grow.

Can you believe God attends you with the same kind of care? Unhurried and attentive? Beholding you in loving contemplation?

When the motivation is love, vinedressers gladly invest their time. Yet, love is not just the motivation behind good vinedressing, it is the method and the means as well. Love is the founding principle of God's vineyard.

As we walk with Dave through these vineyards in the pages ahead, we'll catch glimpses of our Father Vinedresser—nurturing his branches with patient, attentive care that reflect the values of the kingdom. This is what we'll call the *Flourishing Approach*: a vision of growth grounded in relational depth, sustainability, and alignment with the natural rhythms of creation. It stands in direct contrast to the *Productivity-Driven Approach* with its obsession with speed, productivity, and control. God's way of cultivation doesn't just diverge slightly from this approach, it disrupts the entire foundational assumptions of it.

Flourishing Approach vs. *Productivity-Driven Approach*:

Let's look at a side-by-side comparison of the differences between these two value systems:

Flourishing Approach	Productivity-Driven Approach
Quality	Quantity
Process	Product
Relational responsiveness	System efficiency
Interdependence	Independence
Collaboration	Hierarchy
Empowerment	Control
Long-term sustainability	Quick yields
Cyclical rhythms aligned with creation	Linear growth aimed at profit and scale
Diversity as an asset	Diversity as a threat to efficiency
Rest as essential to sustainability	Rest as an obstacle to progress
Contemplation	Exploitation

Why does this matter?

Because whether we realize it or not, we are constantly being shaped by the value systems of the culture around us. If we're not paying attention, we'll find ourselves formed more by the pressures of productivity than by the pace of the kingdom. We must stay alert to where cultural values diverge from God's way—and continually realign ourselves with the loving approach of our Father, the Vinedresser.

Pause for a moment and consider:

- Which of these approaches has most shaped you?

- Where have you noticed a *Productivity-Driven Approach* show up in your work, relationships, and faith communities?

- What will it take to embrace the *Flourishing Approach* of God's kingdom instead?

This kind of change doesn't happen overnight. Like the kingdom, it starts small and grows slowly through little choices we make to embrace a different vision.

Changing Culture—One Vineyard at a Time

When Dave moved back to Old Mission Peninsula from Napa Valley in 2017, he had a dream to transform the local farming industry through organic, relational, and sustainable practices indicative of *the Flourishing Approach*. In a culture largely shaped by industrial farming which prizes productivity and efficiency, this approach is anything but conventional.

Yet, by helping farmers and vineyard owners observe how vines are naturally designed to grow in interdependent relationships and adopt methods that work *with* nature instead of against it,

Dave has quietly been changing the culture—one vineyard at a time.

Take, for example, a thirty-acre field that Dave has been transforming from a cherry orchard into a vineyard on Old Mission Peninsula. For several years, Dave has been partnering with the landowners to prepare the ground—not by rushing to plant vines, but by layering rounds of cover crops that enrich the soil with nutrients. "I'll keep planting different cover crops over and over until it's ready to plant," he tells me. "Because the whole process is building health into the soil. If you look at the relational wholeness between soil and grapevines, it's magnificent. The cover crops release nutrients that feed the microbes, which in turn feed the vine's roots."

As I step onto the field of freshly plowed earth, my shoe sinks into the soft earth. I kneel, scooping up a handful of soil, and it falls to the ground in moist clumps. This is holy ground. Hidden from sight, this soil is rich with a diverse community of billions of microorganisms teeming with life.

Unlike industrial farming, which extracts as much as possible from the land in the shortest amount of time, Dave and the vineyard owners are investing in what can't yet be seen: the microbial life beneath the surface and the biodiverse web of interdependent relationships that will one day support the vine.

This process will take years, and they may never fully see the fruit of their labor, but that's not the point. Their work is motivated by a love for the entire community of creation in the vineyard for decades to come. In many ways, this mirrors Indigenous wisdom, which teaches that the decisions we make today should be shaped by their impact seven generations from now.

In a world obsessed with speed and scale, what does it mean to be shaped by the slow, loving hands of a Vinedresser? One who tends the hidden life beneath the soil of our souls with a long-term vision?

What if he's less concerned with quick results and more invested in the deep, unseen work of lasting health and transformation—in you and in your community?

Lauren and the Pruned Vine

In the introduction, I mentioned the painting I was working on when I first met Dave. I was asked to paint the pruned vine from John 15 for our ministry staff conference. The theme was *Seeking God for Revival*, and as I painted, I had a sense that the pruned vine had something to teach me, and us, about revival and how it comes. A week later, as I studied the source images I had taken and started painting the outline of the vine, I got a text.

"Lauren is in a coma. Please pray."

Lauren Markel was a close friend and colleague. She had been battling DIPG (an inoperable brain tumor) for 4 years, and now was in the battle for her life.

At that moment, my soul hit a fork in the road. Should I keep painting?

There was a part of me that wanted to stop. Not because I needed to stop in order to grieve or pray, but because it would have been easier to escape that way. I wanted to flee into busyness. To flee into numbing through controlling my environment and mindlessly blasting through my inbox. The war between *the Productivity-Driven Approach* and *the Flourishing Approach* was already raging within me.

But there, within my office, as I held my brush in my hand and read the text message with the news about my friend, there was a beckoning in my spirit that said, "keep going."

The chaotic thoughts and confusion, pain, and questions needed to be funneled into the river of prayer through creating. There was no other way they could come out. I needed to paint a way through the ache, and the path took the form of a pruned vine that wept for her, that wept for all of us that felt the sting of the curse that day.

And so, as I painted shadows and light and creases within the vine—bending and twisting towards the sky—there was a rightness about it. A sense of confidence that yes, this is what I need to be doing right now.

Not work emails or phone calls or finishing up other projects. Not even journaling my prayers or kneeling in lament. For this moment, this was my work. And it was holy work.

My brush and paint became a channel for unleashing all the uncertainty, the sadness, the prayers welling up and spilling over in the stormy blue shade of Payne's Grey. With the force of color and movement and form, the grief made its way out into the pruned vine stripped bare of the glory of fruitfulness.

What remained on the vine was raw and exposed weakness and vulnerability. The water droplets pregnant with paint rained down the clayboard, holding within them the weight of waiting and the gravity of time.

Would she die or would she live?

The next day, on October 25th, 2019, I joined a 24-hour virtual prayer vigil to pray for Lauren's healing while she was still in a coma. I took the first slot from 1–2pm. While I was painting and praying, I felt God invite me to dance. It felt awkward at first, but as I danced, I pictured Lauren and the joy she experienced when dancing in worship. Lauren loved to dance. She frequently roped our staff team into Nintendo Wii Just Dance™ parties at the end of long-day conferences. She was the one scoring all the points, her head tilted back in a laugh with her beautiful giant smile beaming towards the ceiling.

Later, I found that it was at 2pm when Lauren passed. I just knew in my bones—I had started dancing the moment she was dancing with Jesus.

Returning to the Vine

When I returned to the painting the next day, the vine stood there silent as death and brooding with the color of loss. It was uncomfortable to look at because it was the visual truth that was too raw and vulnerable to name.

It just stood there testifying defiantly against any attempt to fix the situation. Any attempt to rush on towards hope or resolution was pulled back with the weight of the vine—its roots pressing forcefully toward the depths.

I thought back to my time with Dave in the vineyard and imagined God contemplating Lauren with the same tender attentiveness. Then my mind went to what Lauren had taught me about abiding in Jesus. John 15 was her life passage—one she had studied deeply during her sabbatical and shared passionately with anyone who would listen.

In one of her prayer letters, she wrote, "when you abide in the vine and spend time with Jesus, you will bear much fruit. In Sabbatical, the truth of John 15 has soaked into the depths of who I am and I will never be the same coming back to campus ministry."

A few years later, in the last year of her life, Lauren was too weak to even leave her home. If someone looked at that time purely from a *Productivity-Driven Approach*, one might say Lauren was not fruitful. There was no outward display of strength or achievement in her last days. The growth chart of her ministry was definitely not going up and to the right.

But Lauren knew, as Dave does, that fruit ripens from a healthy relationship between vine, vinedresser, and branches. Ministry for her began with abiding in Jesus, the True Vine. And Lauren's connection to Jesus was strong. In one conversation as her health was declining, she told me, "my body is weak, but my spirit is strong." Indeed, she was stronger than most people I knew.

Her leaves had fallen off and she was wilting, but like a branch at the end of harvest, she soaked up all the light she could in Jesus and channeled it down into the roots of prayer and worship, seeking him for revival for all of us. Like Dave, Lauren saw her work now as building into the soil for generations to come. Even though the fruit was hard to see during her last days, I can only imagine what kind of harvest we are gathering now from her prayers several years ago.

Lauren perceived something we often fail to notice when we live from a *Productivity-Driven Approach*: how resurrection really comes. Revival doesn't come out of our human strength and striving toward external metrics of fruit, but out of an inner strength and dependence on the only one who can bring resurrection.

And this was a lesson our staff would soon need to learn.

Pruning as a Pathway to Revival

Several months after Lauren's passing, at our staff conference, the *Pruned Vine* painting stood just outside the conference room doors, welcoming the gaze of each participant as they made their way to the main sessions. It was January 2020, and we didn't know then how its brooding presence was like a prophetic sign of what was to come.

Just weeks later, the COVID-19 pandemic forced our staff off campus. The ministry, like most ministries during that time, dwindled in size. A friend admitted to me later, *"That painting was hard to look at. It reminded me too much of death. But, now I see how prophetic it was and what God was preparing us for."*

The pandemic became a season of painful pruning. It exposed how many of us, myself included, had been operating with a *Productivity-Driven Approach* to ministry. Yet, even in that stripping away, we were invited to return to our roots—to abide in Jesus and reimagine ministry through the lens of a loving Vinedresser.

It was as if God was whispering through Dave's words, *"I'm going to do everything in my power to cultivate you back to health."*

As the potential for fruit was cut back for a time, God began to show many of us that his deepest concern is not what we produce, but who we are becoming. The COVID-19 season reminded us that sometimes, the most important growth is what happens underground where we cannot see.

Fruitfulness, we learned, doesn't always look like large numbers and impressive programs.

It doesn't trend on social media or make headlines. It may never hit the cover of *Forbes, Time,* or even *Christianity Today.*

But it looks like Lauren's life; one that is deeply rooted in Jesus, the True Vine. It looks like faithful dependence on God, mutual interdependence with one another, and connection with the land itself.

Digging Deeper:

1. Think about the difference between the values and methods of *the Flourishing Approach* and *the Productivity-Driven Approach*. How have you been shaped by either of these ways of life?

2. How has this impacted your view of God?

3. How does Lauren's story challenge your view of fruitfulness?

Notes

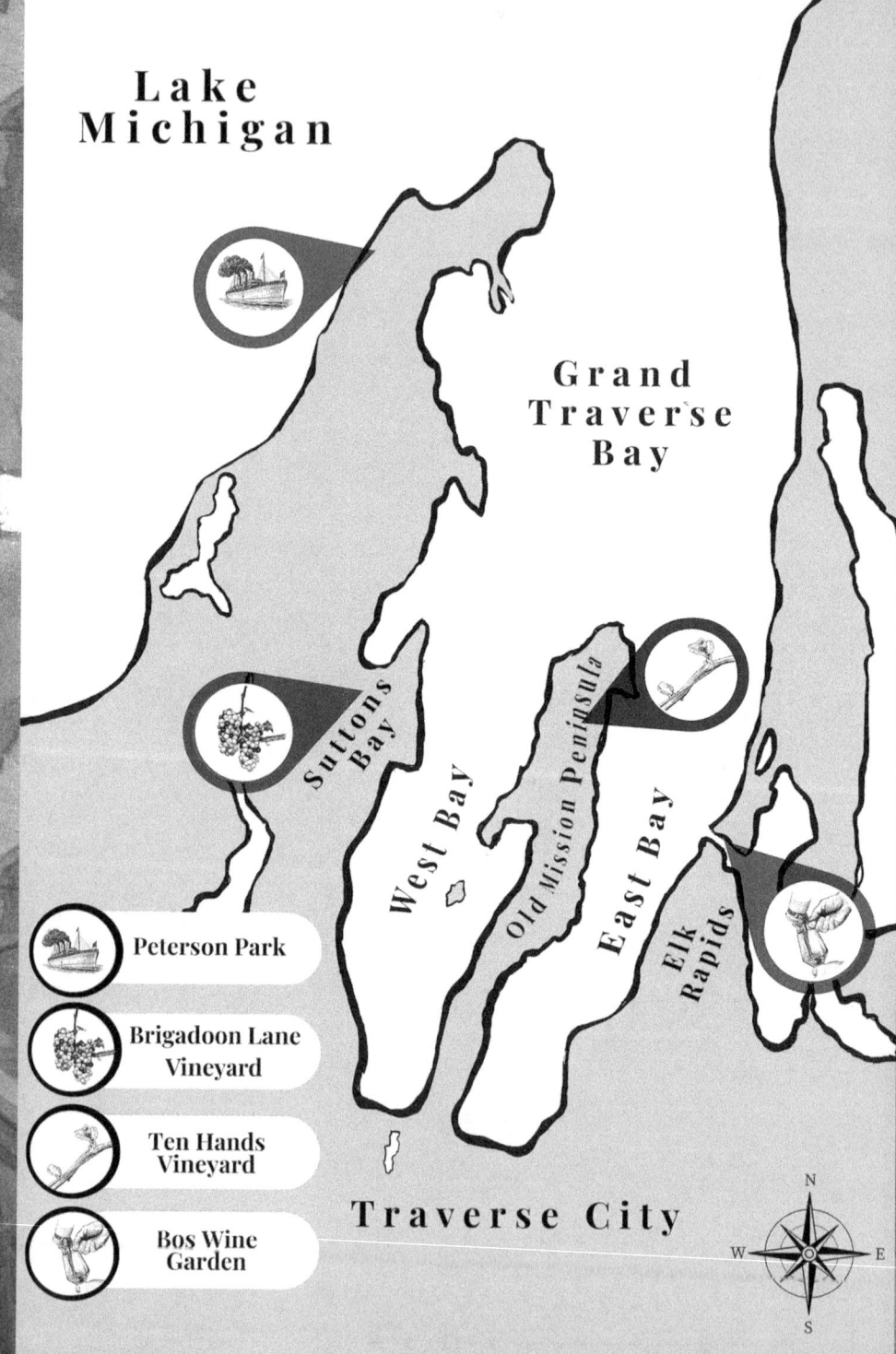

Chapter 2:

Terroir

"I will sing for the one I love
a song about his vineyard:
My loved one had a vineyard
on a fertile hillside.
He dug it up and cleared it of stones
and planted it with the choicest vines."
Isaiah 5:1–2

I've never minded the thirty-five-minute drive to meet Dave in the vineyards on Old Mission Peninsula. Time seems to slip by as I weave between the southern shore of Grand Traverse West Bay and downtown Traverse City. On this early April day, the beach volleyball courts are still empty along the shore, and the water is calm, but alive in the sun.

As I head north up the peninsula, glimpses of East Bay flash through the trees. The last of the snow has melted, revealing strips of pale sand and stony shoreline. It is prime hunting ground for Petoskey stones—fossilized coral that reemerge in the shallows with the spring thaw. Roadside stands sit vacant for now, but soon they'll overflow with tart cherries, tomatoes, jams, zucchini, and lavender.

Climbing one of the many rolling hills on the peninsula, the landscape expands into a panoramic view of vineyards spilling down to the bay, and I take a deep breath. There is something magical about this place.

The vineyards on the peninsula are situated just below the 45th parallel, a latitude known among vintners as a kind of "golden latitude" due to the favorable conditions for viticulture. The long summer days and cool nights allow the grapes to ripen slowly and develop depth and complexity in flavor. This special latitudinal line runs through some of the world's most celebrated wine regions—Bordeaux and the Rhône Valley in France, Piedmont in Italy, and Oregon's Willamette Valley.

When I spot the familiar red roof of the Old Mission General Store near the tip of the peninsula, I turn onto Happy Hour Lane, a narrow dirt road flanked by Vineyard 15 and Ten Hands Vineyard. Dave is already among the rows of Blaufränkisch vines, ready to introduce me to the unique setting of these vines.

He begins where all good stories do: in the soil.

"Here, we have sandy limestone soil that drains quickly," Dave says, "When we get a big rainstorm, water runs right through, so the vines aren't sitting in mud."

At the edge of the vineyard, I gaze out toward East Bay, stretched in quiet repose across the horizon.

"Even though we're in a cool-climate region," Dave explains, "the surrounding water creates a microclimate. It warms slowly, but holds that warmth late into the season, which is great for vines that bud and ripen late like Pinot Noir, Riesling, and Chardonnay, yielding wines with high acidity, complexity, and delicate profiles."

He points back to the slope behind us. "You wouldn't think anything of this subtle incline, but about the third week of September, the cooler air by the bay slows sugar accumulation in the vines below."

He goes on to explain, "Everything in the vine's surrounding environment influences the kind of fruit it grows. Even the same variety of grape planted here will taste noticeably different than the one planted just down the road."

Vinters have a word for this: *terroir*. The French term, pronounced *ter-WAHR*, refers to the way a wine's taste and quality is shaped by its surrounding context.

Dave puts it this way:

> You could blindfold me and take me to my Grandma's house, and just by the smell, I would know where I am, though I might not be able to identify the exact scent. For vines, it's the sandy limestone soil, the fact that it's on a ridge between two bays, and the shifting sunlight and rainfall. It's the way plants interact with each other and the mysterious symbiotic relationship between microbes, bacteria, fungi, and roots. God has designed the world to be complex, yet highly relational. Terroir is how all these interconnected relationships within the vine's environment shape it into what it becomes.

Terroir teaches us something profound: *our formation is deeply tied to place.*

• ○ •

Terroir: The way a wine uniquely reflects the context in which a vine grows from year to year.

4 Primary Influences on Terroir: soil, climate, landscape, and **tradition** (the particular cultivation practices of a vinedresser, often passed down from generation to generation, such as pruning techniques, canopy management, and harvest timing).

• ○ •

Every story unfolds in a setting, and ours is no different. In the vineyard, terroir—the unique combination of soil, climate, and landscape—is not just a backdrop; it's an active character in the story, working in concert with the vinedresser to shape the vine.

Likewise, our lives consist of countless factors that the Vinedresser works with to nurture who we grow to become. Embedded within the soil of our stories are layers of cultural and family history, the nourishment we receive from our spiritual community, the things we absorb on social media, and even the food we eat, just to name a few.

We are also shaped by broader forces like the political climate, cultural landscape, and the geography we inhabit. Like a vine's terroir, these elements leave an imprint on our character and influence the unique fruit we bear.

When I talked with my dad, David Lau, about terroir, he was intrigued by the idea. As he spent time mulling it over, he defined it this way in his own poetic language:

Terroir—the distinctive grounding of locale (proxemics) and time (temporality)—an anchoring of place and time—where and when the wine began.

Terroir connects us to our presence, our grounding in place and the here-and-now of time—something larger than ourselves. Terroir suggests our distinctive connection to the earth. It's what weds us here. It shows us we belong.

In contrast, lostness refers to disoriented-ness. It refers to no longer knowing where we are. When we are lost, we lose sight of our sense of what's important, really important. The more we become lost, the more we lose our connectedness to all that's outside us as well as the seen and unseen of what's within. We fail to see our value to others, our value to the world, our value to ourselves.

Many of us, particularly in westernized contexts, have this unsettling sense of lostness, of being deeply *displaced*. Our connection to the land is often fractured or unclear.

Finding Terroir

Walter Brueggemann describes it well: "The sense of being lost, displaced, and homeless is pervasive in contemporary culture. The yearning to belong somewhere, to have a home, to be in a safe place, is a deep and moving pursuit ... increasing numbers of persons are disoriented, characterized as possessors of the 'homeless mind.'"[1]

Though we are shaped by our environment, we may feel alienated from it, as if we're living on land that doesn't know our name,

---

1. Walter Brueggemann, *The Land: Place as Gift, Promise, and Challenge in Biblical Faith*, 2nd ed. (Minneapolis: Fortress Press, 2002), 1.

or we its. Robin Wall Kimmerer calls it "species loneliness"[2]: a deep sadness stemming from estrangement from the rest of creation, from the loss of relationship. Due to colonization, many of us live on land that is not native to us, either as displaced people or as those whose ancestors displaced others.

Industrialization has further widened this gap—where Indigenous communities and traditional farmers once worked in relationship with the land, now agricultural machines and factories process our food. Modern technology and the ease of air travel have made it possible to move anywhere, yet this freedom often leaves us feeling like nomads looking for a place to call home.

In addition, rising violence, abusive political regimes, and other destabilizing forces have displaced countless people, turning them into refugees in search of a safe place to put down roots. As of June 2024, 122.6 million people have been forcibly displaced from their homes due to violence, threat, and persecution.[3] As we have become more transient and fragmented, our sense of belonging—to land, to community, and even to ourselves—feels increasingly out of reach.

Yet, for better or worse, this is the world in which we find ourselves. This is part of the terroir that is forming us. So, how do we cultivate a sense of belonging if we are not native to where we live?

Jesus, the True Vine, offers a way forward.

---

2. Robin Wall Kimmerer, *Braiding Sweetgrass: Indigenous Wisdom, Scientific Knowledge, and the Teachings of Plants* (Minneapolis: Milkweed Editions, 2013), 207.

3. United Nations High Commissioner for Refugees (UNHCR), *Refugee Data Finder*, accessed April 28, 2025, https://popstats.unhcr.org/refugee-statistics.

Abiding in the True Vine

When Jesus refers to himself as the "vine" in John 15, his hearers would have recalled the passage in Psalm 80, how God transplanted his vine (Israel) from Egypt and planted it in the Promised Land, their true terroir. But by Jesus' time, the people of Israel had experienced exile, oppression under foreign rulers, and an ongoing longing for restoration. Even those who had returned to Jerusalem still lived under Roman occupation, caught between the hope of belonging and the harsh reality of displacement.

Into this tension, Jesus declares, "I am the true vine." No longer is Israel's identity rooted in land or national heritage, it is now found as we abide in him. One of the definitions for this word *abide*, used frequently in John 15, is "to dwell and be held, kept continually."[4] It is a word that conveys a sense of home and belonging; the feeling of being held and kept in the care of someone who loves you.

Jesus tells us here that wherever we put down our roots, we can find belonging when we are held continually by him, the True Vine. The people of God are no longer tied to a particular territory, but to the person of Jesus.

However, having a spiritual home in Christ doesn't sever our connection to the land, as some have understood it. This theology looks more like escapism. *If heaven is our true home and one day we'll "fly away, oh glory," then what does the land matter?*

Perhaps our sense of dislocation stems from how we have misinterpreted Jesus' words here. Revelation 21 gives us a picture of heaven coming down to earth, not us escaping up to heaven.

---

4. "G3306 – *menō* – Strong's Greek Lexicon (NIV)," *Blue Letter Bible,* accessed February 4, 2025, https://www.blueletterbible.org/lexicon/g3306/niv/mgnt/0-1/.

Romans 8 reminds us that creation itself will one day be liberated *with* the children of God.[5] We are more deeply connected to creation and the land than we know.

Jesus himself lived an incarnational life—fully embodied and intimately connected to the people and place where he lived. So, when he says he is the True Vine, he doesn't mean our belonging in him is somehow found *apart* from our context in some abstract spiritual way, but *within it*.

His invitation isn't escapism, it is to reclaim a way of being that is deeply rooted, wherever we are planted. In a world that is fragmented by mobility and displacement, the call to settle into the land—to invest in a place—is a radical act of incarnation.

Whether we are digital nomads or live all of our lives in the soil of our ancestors, cultivating *terroir*—an awareness of how place shapes us—calls us to be agents of reconciliation in our fractured relationship with the land and its people.

We are called not just to "do ministry" but to *be planted*, to humbly invest in the flourishing of the land, the community of creation, and the people in our local community. This begins by learning the stories of the place we inhabit and discerning how our lives are woven into the story already unfolding there.

Just as vinedressers draw out the character of the land to craft a wine that tells its story, we, too, are invited to attend to our relationship with the land and allow it to shape the narrative of our lives.

---

5. Romans 8:19–22.

Listening to the Story of the Land

Since moving to Traverse City in 2017, I've been on a journey to learn the story of this place as I sink my roots into the sandy limestone soil.

Long before we arrived, glaciers moved like slow plows across this region, carving deep grooves that eventually melted into the Great Lakes. As the ice descended south along what would become Lake Michigan, it split like lungs into two sections, forming East and West Grand Traverse Bay. Between them, it left a slender stretch of land, now called Old Mission Peninsula, rising like a sternum between the bays.

It was the Anishinaabek who first stewarded this land—the Ojibwe (Chippewa), Odawa (Ottawa), and Potawatomi nations, collectively known as the Three Fires Confederacy. They've taught me the most about how to pay attention to the unique story of this place.

Their relationship with the land is marked by generosity, gratitude, and reciprocity. They have shown me how to cherish the sacred gifts of the entire community of creation that calls this place home; the Maple Trees that offer their sweet sap for syrup, the Birch trees that sway in the wind, and the Trillium erupting into silent glory on the forest floor in spring. Their connection to water, the rhythms of the seasons, and the stories embedded in the land still reverberate across the landscape—from the ancient dunes shaped by glaciers to the cool shores where Petoskeys hide.

Yet, this sacred relationship was violently disrupted. In the 1830s and 40s, treaties were signed under duress, forcibly removing the Anishinaabek from their ancestral lands. The 1836 Treaty of Washington ceded millions of acres, including this region, to the United States government. Some resisted, but much was taken.

Among the settlers who arrived in the wake of that disruption were my husband's ancestors. In 1867, the Garthe family (his maternal ancestors) journeyed from Norway, seeking a new life. Their ticket was for Chicago, but when they reached the long, slender bays of Grand Traverse, with their steep forested edges and deep, cool waters, it reminded them of the fjords of home. So, they dropped anchor near what is now **Peterson Park (marked on the map)**—once called Garthe Park—and began a new chapter. They made their home among the hills and orchards of Northport and Suttons Bay and became cherry farmers. Many of their descendants have remained here ever since.

As cherry orchards expanded, so did the need for seasonal labor. Migrant workers, first from the southern U.S. and later from Mexico, arrived to assist with labor-intensive harvest. One of my friends, Lila, is deeply connected to that story—her father was one of those cherry pickers. When she visited last summer, we shared this beautiful connection of our intertwined roots.

By the 1970s, settlers discovered that the region's terroir was also ideal for vineyards, which started popping up all along the shores of the bays. It wasn't long before Traverse City transformed into a seasonal hub, pulsing in and out with tourists, turning it into the "Cherry Capital of the World." In summer, the lakes are filled with speedboats and the ground with pop-up festival tents. In winter, they withdraw like the tide, leaving the navy blue bay to crystalize silently into ice caps along the shore.

For years, my husband and I were among these seasonal visitors. We traveled to Suttons Bay to visit his family, but in 2017, the land drew us back for good. The vibrant blue bays began to stretch my soul wide open. Each glimpse of the bay feels like a deep breath, anchoring me in the present moment. Whether it's the small peekaboo views on my way to the grocery store or the vast, shimmering expanse as I approach downtown, the water feels like home.

When I travel downstate, I feel landlocked, as if my soul is suffocating. A friend once pointed out, *"That makes sense, Bette. Just look at your paintings. You've always painted seascapes—you've always been drawn to water."*

As I seek to make my home here, I feel the tension of the many layers of stories still present in the soil: the deep grooves from glaciers turned into lakes, the stewardship of the Anishinaabek, the injustice of displacement, and the presence of migrant workers who still work these fields among vinedressers like Dave.

Like the vines, I am not native here. Yet over time, this place has grafted me into its story—into a family that crossed an ocean to settle here, into a place surrounded by vines, cherry trees, and water, and into a history of hope, loss, and belonging. The Father Vinedresser is helping me pay attention to these stories, so that the fruit of my life might carry the flavor of both the land's story and my own.

Two Different Approaches to Terroir

In the previous chapter, we explored how the vinedresser sets the culture of the vineyard. One way a vinedresser does this is through their approach to *terroir*.

As Tom Petzold, the previous owner of Ten Hands Vineyard, puts it:

> Just as important to terroir as the soil and climate are the people who farm the land—their attitudes, their practices, and their commitment to the long-term health of the vines. Over time, these factors shape the grapes, layering them with the complexity and character of a particular context.

When a winemaker respects the terroir of the grapes, they cultivate a wine that reflects all of this.[6]

The Flourishing Approach to Terroir

In a *Flourishing Approach* to vinedressing and winemaking, there's joy and pride in crafting a wine that tells the story of a specific time and place. Dave points to Northern Michigan Rieslings, as an example:

> Here, on Old Mission Peninsula, even compared to Leelanau just across the bay, our Rieslings pick up the unique flavor note of fennel seed. Many Rieslings in Northern Michigan also carry hints of lemon balm and lemon oil from the soil. But beyond taste, Michigan wines have a delicacy and structure that, when done right, really shine. In winemaking, I am not trying to control the wine, but allow the grapes to express themselves.

And isn't that what God does with us? Rather than controlling us, he desires the fruit we bear to naturally express the unique physical, spiritual, and social terroir of where we grow.

As my wine-loving friend, Bethany, puts it, winemakers who take a *Flourishing Approach* to wine "submit themselves to the land's limitations and create wine with nuance. Those wines invite you to pay attention."

The Productivity-Driven Approach to Terroir

Not all vinedressers and winemakers embrace this philosophy. In the *Productivity-Driven Approach*, winemakers cater to consumers who want consistent wine every time, regardless of when or where it's purchased. Like Starbucks or McDonald's, the goal is

---

6. Tom Petzold, interview with the author, used with permission.

predictability—a wine that tastes the same. Grapes are often sourced from multiple locations and blended to create a uniform product. In this model, terroir isn't a gift, it's a liability.

The efficiency needed for mass production outweighs the messy, intimate, and relational work required to showcase a vine's unique context. When a vine's terroir is ignored, its wine may still be "good," but it loses its personality. Stripped of story, place, and relationship, its memory doesn't stay with us. It becomes a product, not a witness.

Similarly, when we're shaped by systems that disconnect us from our relationship to the land and our particular backgrounds, we lose something. Many churches that operate from this perspective create uniform programs designed for scalability and end up churning out replicas of the same style of disciple.

These systems tend to reflect and reward the values of dominant culture, which means that cultural expressions from minority communities are often overlooked or suppressed.

When the value is for uniformity over uniqueness, our distinctiveness gets flattened. As a result, the rich stories rooted in our ethnicity, family history, traditions, and physical context can be stripped away. We might "fit in," but we don't truly flourish, especially when the cost of belonging is the erasure of who we really are. As a result, we end up yielding cheap bottles of wine devoid of the unique makeup of our community.

Finding My Soul's Terroir

I've had to wrestle with this in my own story, not in the way that many marginalized peoples have, but in quieter ways as my soul has sometimes been constrained by dominant cultural values. As someone who comes from majority culture, my heritage often aligns with what is affirmed and rewarded in society. That alignment brings certain privileges, but it can also make it harder to discern what is truly mine versus what I've unconsciously absorbed.

I was shaped by the soil of my German and Flemish-speaking Belgian ancestors. My mom's side of the family, the "determined Germans," was a gritty kind of soil that formed me into a direct communicator and hard worker. Within the soil of my mom's leadership, my sisters and I became captains of our sports' teams and were awarded for our work ethic and independence. In a culture obsessed with performance, this drive fits easily into systems that reward output.

But I was also nourished by the gentler soil of my dad's lineage of Flemish-speaking Belgians who were incredibly artistic, contemplative, and had a profound connection to creation. I grew up watching my dad slowly sip his coffee at the kitchen table as he wrote poetry, the morning sun pouring over his back, and his vegetable garden sprawling behind him out the picture window. His childhood was spent racing down the sand dunes of Lake Michigan and body surfing in the waves.

His contemplative ways and deep connection to water formed me in ways I didn't realize until much later. Like my dad, I thrive when I can stretch out my thoughts in solitude—moving in rhythm with creation, my feet pressing into shifting sand as I gaze out at the water for hours in quiet contemplation.

These two lineages—the driven and contemplative—often wrestle within me. Honoring my *terroir* means allowing both to nourish who I am becoming. The Vinedresser is teaching me that there is more to me than my ability to get things done. He also delights in the artist within me, the part that moves slowly, listens deeply, and resists cookie-cutter molds. Abiding in the Vine means letting all parts of myself emerge, not just the parts our culture rewards.

As I've learned to name and honor my own terroir, I've also come to see how important it is to make space for the terroir of others, especially those in cultures who have been historically sidelined or overlooked.

While my heritage has been largely affirmed by dominant culture, many have had to fight to simply express or preserve their own. This awareness has invited me to become a more attentive listener and faithful witness to the richness of stories that differ from mine. For a vineyard to flourish, it depends on all of us tending to the diversity of soil we've come from, and learning how our stories can nourish one another.

Celebrating the Soil of Our Terroir

This is the kind of cultivation the Vinedresser employs in the vineyard of his kingdom. In Revelation, we see a picture of every tribe, tongue, and nation, worshiping around the throne—not in uniformity, but in the unique expression of their languages and cultures.[7] God is not after mass-produced, one-size-fits-all kinds of disciples. His approach is much more intentional, where each life bears fruit, shaped by the soil from which it came.

As we surrender to the Vinedresser's care, even the overlooked parts of our heritage can become fertile ground for beautiful fruit. Flourishing means allowing these parts of ourselves to find their truest expression. Like the Michigan Rieslings that carry hints of fennel or lemon balm, the fruit of our lives begins to take on the flavor of where we come from and where we are now. And that is fruit worth celebrating.

---

7. Revelation 7:9.

When we abide in the Vine, we don't lose ourselves; we become more fully who we were created to be. Our uniqueness isn't erased, it's brought to life.

Digging Deeper:

1. What is your current terroir like? What is your surrounding physical, spiritual, cultural, and emotional environment and how is it shaping you?

2. Rather than blending in through uniformity, how might your life become a celebration of the gifts your background carries?

3. How can you honor the history of the land where you live? What might it look like to allow it to shape you? To learn more about the indigenous peoples native to your region, visit https://native-land.ca/

Notes

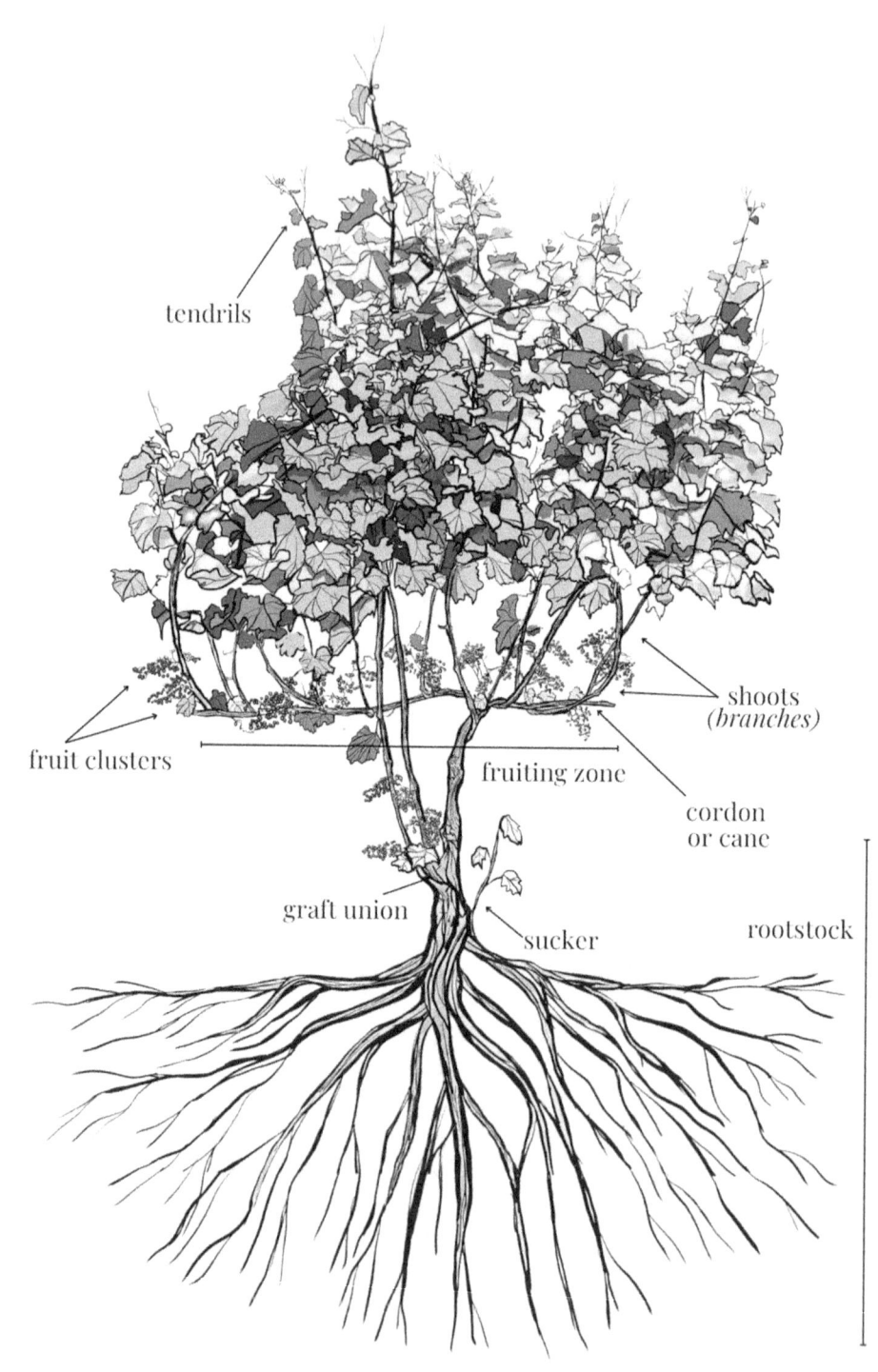

tendrils

fruit clusters

shoots
(*branches*)

fruiting zone

cordon
or cane

graft union

sucker

rootstock

Chapter 3:

The Vine and Branches

• O •

"I am the vine; you are the branches.
If you remain in me and I in you,
you will bear much fruit; apart from me
you can do nothing."
John 15:5

Dave and I stood in a vineyard on Old Mission Peninsula between rows of vines at the end of harvest. As we looked down a row of Merlot vines nodding off to sleep after a hard season's work, I asked, "What do you think Jesus was referring to when he said he is the vine, and we are the branches?"

Dave reached down and grabbed the sturdy trunk of the vine, its base disappearing underground into the roots, his fingers several inches apart.

"This is the vine," he said.

Then he reached up and gently wrapped his fingers around two lateral cane branches, no larger than a drumstick, stretched along the trellis.

"And these are the branches. The vines in Jesus' day were probably head-trained, more like a bush than what you see here. But the principle is the same: the branches grow out from the center, from the vine. Every year, they are pruned, grow, and produce fruit, but the vine remains the same."

As I've walked these rows with Dave over the years, the vine has slowly begun to reveal its secrets. In its sacred rhythms, I've glimpsed an unspoken exchange between vine and branches—a silent communion of giving and receiving.

In winter, when its stark silhouette rests bare against the snow, the veteran vine whispers to its branches about resilience, patience, and surrender.

In spring, as sleeping branches awaken in tender green, they buzz excitedly about a burst of energy found in the vine's deep roots. As their leaves flatten out, they soak up the energy of the sun and return it back to the vine.

In summer, when excess shoots are cut away and I watch them quickly wither once severed from the source, they cry out their dependence on the vine—for water, for nourishment, for life.

And in autumn, when the branches sag beneath the weight of ripened fruit, the vine bears them up with a self-giving strength—a power that holds, supports, and gives itself away, even as the branches pour themselves out in the fruit.

Abiding and Attachment

In *The Other Half of Church*, Michel Hendricks and Dr. Jim Wilder describe this connection between the vine and branches through the lens of attachment. They write, "The image of a vine and branch is a clear picture of attachment. We have an attachment to Jesus that bears fruit in our lives (character change). He presents a simple formula: no attachment, no fruit. Through the Father's attachment to Jesus, divine love flows to us through our connection to the vine."[1]

Attachment theory is a concept rooted in neuroscience and psychology.[2] Research has shown that we are biologically wired for connection. From birth, we form deep relational bonds with our caregivers when they respond consistently to our cries for help and offer what we need. These attachments create lasting neural pathways that endure, even in their absence or in conflict.

This idea took on deeper meaning for me when I learned how new branches are connected to a vine through grafting. If you want to grow a particular variety of grape, you don't plant it from seed, you graft it onto an established rootstock.

Through a careful and intentional process, the branch is cut and bound to another vine. Over time, their tissues fuse. The grafted

---

1. Michel Hendricks and Jim Wilder, *The Other Half of Church: Christian Community, Brain Science, and Overcoming Spiritual Stagnation* (Colorado Springs: Moody Publishers, 2020), 87.

2. For a deeper understanding of attachment and its neurological underpinnings, see Daniel J. Siegel, *The Developing Mind: How Relationships and the Brain Interact to Shape Who We Are*, 3rd ed. (New York: Guilford Press, 2020).

branch becomes fully integrated into the life of the vine, drawing strength and nourishment as if it had always belonged.

In many ways, this is a picture of how relational attachment works. Hendricks and Wilder describe attachment as "a life-giving forever bond with no mechanism in the brain to unglue us."[3] Just as a grafted branch is permanently joined to the vine and becomes a part of its life, we are joined to Christ in a secure, enduring connection.

While not all human attachments are healthy or secure, the attachment we have to Christ, the True Vine, is. Just as a child doesn't need to strive to earn acceptance and belonging in a family with attentive parents, we don't need to strive to abide in Christ. Through his work on the cross, we are already grafted in. Our connection is secure, even when God feels distant. As Hendricks and Wilder express, our attachment to Jesus is a "glue with a binding strength that nothing in all creation can break."[4]

So, what kind of fruit flows from *this* kind of attachment?

Bearing the Fruit of Christ's Character

Unlike *the Productivity-Driven Approach*, when Jesus speaks of fruit in John 15, he isn't describing measurable achievements or outward success. He speaks the language of attachment, the language of love:

> If you remain in me and I in you, you will bear much fruit;
> apart from me you can do nothing ...
> This is to my Father's glory, that you bear much fruit,

---

3. Hendricks and Wilder, *The Other Half of Church*, 47.

4. Hendricks and Wilder, *The Other Half of Church*, 88.

showing yourselves to be my disciples.
As the Father has loved me, so have I loved you.
Now remain in my love.[5]

According to Jesus, we cannot grow fruit on our own effort or performance. Fruit comes from abiding. When we remain in Christ, his life flows into ours, producing the fruit of his character—the fruit of the Spirit: "Love, joy, peace, patience, kindness, goodness, faithfulness, gentleness, and self-control."[6]

When my kids were learning the fruits of the Spirit, we'd sing along to "The Fruit of the Spirit" by Uncle Charlie, who playfully reminded us that "the fruit of the Spirit's not a coconut," or "not a grape," a silly way to teach that the fruit isn't just something you can see.[7]

Perhaps we adults need our own version of this song:

"the fruit of the Spirit's not a crowd,"
"not a product,"
"not a promotion,"
"not an applause."

Yet these are the metrics we're tempted to use when we confuse fruitfulness with productivity. Too often, churches and ministries adopt this perspective, prioritizing growth strategies and measurable impact over the slow, relational work of abiding. As Hendricks and Wilder observe, they "operate more like an efficiently run religious institution than a family. They do many good things but may not possess good character."[8]

---

5. John 15:5b, 8–9.

6. Galatians 5:22–23, NLT.

7. Uncle Charlie, "The Fruit of the Spirit," on *Superhero*, 2005.

8. Hendricks and Wilder, *The Other Half of Church*, 93.

And we've all seen this right?

Most of us have been a part of churches or ministries where the focus was on external signs of growth, while the character of its leaders produced the fruit of exploitation or abuse.

Or we've been in meetings where the focus is solely on the desired numerical outcome of a program instead of the formation of the people.

In agricultural terms, this is like measuring a vine's success by its yield while ignoring the health of its roots.

But the fruit of the Spirit can't be rushed or manufactured. It resists our metrics and deadlines. It's cultivated slowly, over time, through secure bonds of attachment. It's not what we produce *for* God but who we become *in* God when we remain in the vine.

Attaching to Christ's Love

So how do we nurture a secure attachment to Christ that bears the fruit of the Spirit?

Paul's prayer for the Ephesians gives us a clue:

> I pray that out of his glorious riches he may strengthen you with power through his Spirit in your inner being, so that Christ may dwell in your hearts through faith. And I pray that you, being *rooted and established in love*, may have power, together with all the Lord's holy people, to grasp how wide and long and high and deep is the love of Christ and *to know* this love that *surpasses knowledge*—that you may be filled to the measure of all the fullness of God.[9]

---

9. Ephesians 3:16-19, (*emphasis mine*).

Paul prays that we would *know* Christ's love—a love that *surpasses* knowledge. But, how do you *know* something that *surpasses* knowledge?

Here, Paul uses two different Greek words for "knowledge":

- *Gnosis* refers to intellectual understanding—facts, reasoning, and concepts. It primarily engages the left side of the brain.[10]

- *Ginōskō*, by contrast, is relational knowledge. It means "to feel, to become known, to understand and perceive."[11] In Jewish culture, it was so intimate a term that it was used as a euphemism for sexual union.

Hendricks and Wilder explain that this type of knowledge involves processes in the brain's right hemisphere—the area responsible for integrating embodied experiences, emotions, identity, and community connection.[12] This experiential and relational understanding shapes our character, reflected in the fruit of the Spirit.

So, in essence, Paul is saying:

> "I want you to *know (ginōskō)* Christ's love in an experiential, relational way that surpasses mere intellectual *knowledge (gnosis).*"

---

10. Strong's Greek Lexicon, s.v. "γνῶσις" (G1108) – *gnōsis* – Blue Letter Bible (NIV), accessed July 14, 2025, https://www.blueletterbible.org.

11. Strong's Greek Lexicon, s.v. "γινώσκω" (G1097) – *ginōskō* – Blue Letter Bible (NIV), accessed January 12, 2024, https://www.blueletterbible.org.

12. Hendricks and Wilder, *The Other Half of Church*, 28.

Experiential Love That Transforms

Here's the key: God's love cannot remain merely an idea to be grasped intellectually to transform us. It must be felt—an embodied, tangible experience that engages our whole being.

Isn't that what God did in the incarnation? His love literally took on flesh so that we might know him, not just in words or theory, but through lived, relational experience.

David Benner puts it beautifully in *Surrender to Love*:

> What we need is a knowing that is deeper than belief. It must be based on experience. ... it comes from sitting at the feet of Jesus, gazing into his face and listening to his assurances of love for me. It comes from letting God's love wash over me, not simply trying to believe it. It comes from soaking in the scriptural assurances of such love, not simply reading them and trying to remember or believe them. It comes from spending time with God, observing how he looks at me. It comes from watching his watchfulness over me and listening to his protestations of love for me.[13]

Christ's love is not a concept to grasp, but a reality to encounter. And it is *that* love—felt, embodied, relational—that transforms us.

Beauty and the Formation of the Soul

A week before Dave and I first met in October 2019, I drove south from Traverse City to the Hermitage Retreat Center in Three Rivers, Michigan, for a group retreat. As my tires crunched over the dirt driveway lined with pines, I passed the familiar

---

13. David G. Benner, *Surrender to Love: Discovering the Heart of Christian Spirituality* (Downers Grove, IL: InterVarsity Press, 2015), 76.

hand-painted brown sign that read, "begin to slow down" and sighed with remembrance.

The Hermitage had been the place where I spent many silent retreat days when I lived just north, in Kalamazoo. On this sacred ground, I had often heard the Spirit's whisper confirming my call. But years had passed since my last visit. Only recently had I learned that my ancestors—immigrants from Germany—had also settled in this very town. That knowledge deepened my sense of connection to the land, as if it were already part of the *terroir* that had formed me.

I arrived early, before the retreat began, and made my way to the spiral labyrinth. It unfurled before me like a fern, its path curling inward through three distinct spirals. The short, green grass stood in sharp contrast to the tall trees circling the valley, ablaze with red and orange.

It occurred to me that I had walked this same labyrinth twice before while pregnant—once with my oldest, Isaiah, and once with my youngest, Winston. But on this particular day, as I was preparing my heart for an upcoming sabbatical, I sensed the Spirit whisper, *"You are pregnant again."*

I knew it in my body as I took those first slow steps into the labyrinth, the timidness. The hesitation to move forward. The vulnerability accompanied by the first few moments of panic, shock, and wonder reeling around in my gut. I walked gingerly. Something was shifting in me—a shift in my soul and my body from which I would never return.

But I wasn't pregnant with a child this time. No, this time, I sensed the Spirit say, *"You are pregnant with me,"* which caught me a bit off guard until, as I took the first few steps into the labyrinth, I experienced in a mysteriously embodied way—what Jesus described in John 15:4: *"Remain in me, as I also remain in you."*

Somehow, I felt in the womb of God. I was in him, and he was in the womb of my spirit, creating something new. I was abiding in him, and he in me. Over the course of the next few days on the retreat, my true self began to arise and unfold from this deeply intimate and vulnerable union.

Beauty and Attachment

The retreat, *Beauty and the Formation of the Soul*, was my first encounter with Dr. Curt Thompson, a psychiatrist and writer known for his work at the intersection of neuroscience, attachment, and spiritual formation.

In his opening lecture, Thompson introduced us to Dr. Dan Siegel's work on attachment. According to Siegel, we develop healthy relational attachments when we experience being seen, soothed, safe, and secure—first with our primary caregivers, and later through expanding circles of connection.

Thompson then explored how beauty plays a role in attachment: "What I most desire is to be seen, known, and desired by the one I desire. Beauty gives us the experience of this with God." When we encounter beauty, he explained, we experience being seen, soothed, safe, and secure by God. This cultivates a secure relational attachment with God, the source of all beauty.

Beauty offers an embodied experience of consummation—union with God himself. As we behold beauty, whether in the brilliance of a sunset or the resonance of Bach's *Cello Suites*, our hearts open to the infinite presence of God. In these sacred moments, he invites us into the Trinitarian dance of attachment between the Vine, the Vinedresser, and the Spirit—like sun and rain that gives life to the vine. This divine dance is also known in the Christian tradition as *perichoresis* which means "mutual indwelling."

Thompson continued, "When we experience being seen, soothed, safe, and secure by God in the presence of beauty, we become more fully alive to who we truly are—the beauty within. And when this beauty shines, we become the true evangelists we are meant to be, shining on a hill."

Then he posed a piercing question: "So why aren't we all shining like a city on a hill?"

He paused.

"In a word: *trauma*."[14]

Trauma and Beauty

Thompson went on, "Trauma disrupts our ability to see and perceive beauty. When we go through trauma, our left and right hemispheres are dis-integrated from one another. Shame is activated in trauma, and it is shame that keeps us from seeing our own beauty and creating new and beautiful things."

These words kept jostling around in my head at the end of the first day. As the car bounded over the bumpy road on the way to my friend's home, I stared out the backseat window of the minivan among friends. Suddenly, it hit me: *shame has kept me from creating.*

For months, I had been asking myself why it was so hard to get into the studio to paint, even when I had the time to do so. Why, even though I longed to create, I hesitated so frequently and put practical things like email and my to-do list in front of this desire.

---

14. Dr. Curt Thompson, remarks from the retreat *Beauty and the Formation of the Soul* at the Hermitage (Three Rivers, MI, 2019), used with permission.

As I began to dig beneath the surface, I began to see where *the Productivity-Driven Approach* had taken root in my soul. Beneath my striving and performing, I uncovered deep wounds of rejection tied to the lie, *"you are not enough."*

Not popular enough.

Not pretty enough.

Not desirable enough.

Not fast enough.

Not good enough.

Not smart enough.

Not male enough.

Since I couldn't control a lot of the reasons I was rejected for not being enough x, y, or z, I channeled my energy into what I could control—my performance, my outputs. I covered the shame of my insufficiencies, and wrapped myself in the fig leaves of my achievements. Maybe, just maybe, if I could prove myself worthy through what I do, I could be loved. I could be desirable. I could be enough.

And it worked. I was noticed and applauded for my hard work. On the swim team in high school, I wasn't the fastest, but I got the "workhorse" award for how hard I practiced. I got As in school not for how smart I was, but for how intensely I studied and completed assignments. In seminary, I worked hard to prove I belonged as a woman there.

When I graduated and went into ministry, I shapeshifted to be whatever version of success my supervisors wanted or needed me to be. I relished the accolades and applause at every stage, forming an unhealthy attachment to the approval of others. But deep down, this reinforced the lie that people only wanted me for what I could do, not for who I was.

What the world seemed to want from me was my efficiency, productivity, and success, not the beauty I created. So when I encountered the pull of *the Productivity-Driven Approach*, my own false self, rooted in my wounds, got sucked into its vortex like a force. At every turn, the true self within me hid in a corner because she was told she didn't belong. And shame kept her there.

When I had this epiphany, I prayed this earnest prayer in my journal that night, *"Jesus, I am asking you to bust down the door of shame and help me to come out. Help my artist soul to awaken and be seen—if only by you at first. Create a holy unfolding in me."*

And the next day, God began answering that prayer with another truth. When Dr. Thompson said it, gravity seemed to double down on me, sinking me into my chair:

"Beauty is the antidote to shame. And beauty is one of God's most effective tools to free us from shame."

Seen, Soothed, Safe, and Secure

As Dr. Thompson proceeded to articulate the role beauty plays in healing and transformation, for the first time in a long time, my true artist self was invited to emerge. She was told she was wanted. She was essential. And there, in that small community room, I began to experience what it felt like to be seen, soothed, safe, and secure in God's embrace as a creator of beauty.

For the first time in a long time, I felt free.

What I began to understand through words were then reinforced by an embodied experience at the retreat center. As I spent time on the grounds reflecting on these things, the curtains of heaven opened with the glow of the setting sun, turning the tall waving grasses into an undulating ocean of gold. Every blade of grass was pregnant with the weight of glory and I knew it.

Everything around me started to illuminate God's presence. I could hear him within the chorus of rustling fall leaves that had burst into persimmon and crimson flame on the edges of the Medieval-style labyrinth on the grounds. As I meditatively walked this labyrinth, every time the path turned toward the center, I felt a wave of beauty hit me palpably, and I gasped out loud. I kept my hand pressed to my chest to steady myself as I sensed his nearness with such gravity that it was hard to take a step.

Later, when we ate our silent meal together around the table, I chewed more slowly. I closed my eyes and savored the lentils in the stew, the warm crisp of the baked bread, and the tartness of the freshly picked apples. In that moment, beauty grounded me in the presence of God.

I cannot overstate how radically transformative this retreat was. Looking back, I can see why: my experience involved a deeply integrated encounter with Jesus. I encountered Jesus through all five senses on the grounds of the retreat center (right brain function), and then Dr. Curt Thompson's teaching gave language to my experience (left brain function). It was a whole-brain, whole-body encounter with God that brought healing.

Like a branch that begins to green and rise towards the trellis from the life force in the roots of the vine, something within me started to arise. In being seen, soothed, safe, and secure—by God, by creation, and by the others at the retreat—I felt myself attaching more securely to the True Vine. I began to unfold into my true self.

Jesus began to replace the lies that I was "not enough" with the truth of my divine identity as an artist created and called by God. I began to experience the re-integration of my brain as beauty began to set me free from shame.

Cultivating a Secure Attachment with Christ, the True Vine

If our thriving and fruitfulness depend on our attachment to the Vine, then we must learn to recognize what threatens that connection.

For vines, disconnection can come from trauma like winter damage or disease. For us, it's often the wounds of our own stories—experiences that, like my own story, may have shaped a way of living that keeps us stuck in shame. And shame, more than anything, can hinder our connection to the True Vine, distancing us from both God and ourselves.

Most of us know the ache of having our true selves trapped behind walls of shame. Perhaps you, too, have believed the lie that the world only values you for what you produce rather than the inherent beauty of who you are. Maybe you hide behind the need to have all the right answers, to be entertaining, to be morally excellent, or to be the faithful friend or the perfect parent.

But there's something deep within all of us that longs to be free.

We all feel it—that quiet ache: the longing to step into the dance of loving attachment with God. The desire to experience and create beauty not as performance, but as communion with him.

When we are held by the Vine, intimately intertwined with his life, we experience what every soul longs for: to be seen, soothed, safe, and secure.

> The vine *sees* the branch's needs and sends life-giving energy where it's needed most.
> The vine *soothes* wounds by pulsing healing sap into areas of pain.
> The vine offers *safely* to the branch, anchoring it through storms and frost.

And the vine offers *security*, empowering the branches to throw out shoots, leaves, and fruit from its stable connection to the vine.

The life of the vine flows into the life of the branch, making them one.

So, when Jesus calls us to remain in him, it's not a demand for performance. It's a compelling invitation into his very life—into a divine dance of communion and co-creation.

For me, this takes the form of painting. For you, it might emerge in the way you prepare a meal, write a line of code, listen to a friend, or build a snow fort with your kids. Whatever shape it takes, when we join him in the dance, we are transformed. And something in the world is transformed too.

Out of that loving union, something beautiful emerges; the fruit of the kingdom of God.

Preparing to Fly

After the retreat ended, I sat on a small wooden bench overlooking a valley, sheltered beneath a simple canopy. As I journaled, my true self rose up to advocate for herself. She began to challenge assumptions that had kept her hidden—assumptions from *the Productivity-Driven Approach* that insisted the world needed my achievements, output, and control.

But, I thought in rebuttal, *"What if my work is play? What if the greatest gift I can offer this anxious system is the beauty I create within it, and even in spite of it? What if the way to diffuse the tension in a Productivity-Driven culture isn't by working with the anxiety by submitting to its demands to produce, but subverting it with unexpected beauty?*

What if instead of working hard to get things done to appease anxiety, I was able to be fully present to beauty—so captivated by Jesus that what is created out of me diffuses anxiety at its source, and brings healing?

In that moment, I saw with piercing clarity that my most valuable contribution to the world was not my achievements, but the overflow of intimacy with God. I knew I experienced the deepest level of attachment to God while creating. My hope was that, when others encountered the fruit of my life, they too would have an experience with God's beauty that transforms.

I paused my journaling when I noticed four woolly bear caterpillars crawling near my feet. Their fuzzy black and orange stripes caught my attention. Later, I learned that woolly bear caterpillars don't spin cocoons right away. Instead, they tuck themselves beneath leaves and logs, hibernating through the harsh winter months. Only in spring do they emerge, taking the stored energy from fall feeding to spin a cocoon and transform into an Isabella Tiger Moth. The waiting, freezing, and stillness of winter is a sacred time of preparation.

I hadn't realized then that these tiny caterpillars were like quiet heralds, foreshadowing my own descent into dormancy. I was coming up on a sabbatical, a season of hiddenness, stillness, and preparation, so I, too, could one day fly.

I closed the retreat with this prayer, one that would prove true in the coming months:

> *Here I am, surrounded by these slowly moving caterpillars.*
> *And now I am beginning to move more slowly —*
> *to digest with intention*
> *all that you will use to form me*
> *from the inside out*

into who you designed me to be:
not just a being of this earth,
but one who can fly.

Digging Deeper:

1. What are some ways you tend to define "fruitfulness?" How is this different from the way it is defined by the fruit of the Spirit?

2. How have you experienced being seen, soothed, safe, and secure in God's love through beauty?

3. How has shame hindered your connection to the True Vine? How has it kept you from seeing your own beauty or creating beautiful things?

Notes

Chapter 4:

The Rhythm

"There is a time for everything,
and a season for every activity under the heavens ...
He has made everything beautiful in its time."
Ecclesiastes 3:1,11

It's early April when I pull onto Brigadoon Lane in Suttons Bay. I follow a narrow, tire-worn path through the grass that's just beginning to turn green. It winds up a hill to a vineyard where Dave is pruning. Rows of vines stretch across the hillside, already clipped back for the season. Pruned clippings lie scattered between the rows as I make my way toward the far end of the vineyard. There, Dave is working on the last few Pinot Gris vines that the migrant workers left untouched for our time together.

Dave greets me with excitement, eager to show me the pruning process. But before we begin, I ask him how he knows it's the right time to start. He pauses for a moment, then says, "In the kind of farming I do, I work with the rhythms of nature. A lot of farmers prefer a cut-and-dry approach, where you mark a calendar with the same dates for pruning and harvest each year. It's more efficient, but it doesn't take into account the condition of the vine or other variables like the timing of seasons that can vary dramatically from year to year."

This is another difference between *the Productivity-Driven Approach* and *the Flourishing Approach*. *The Productivity-Driven Approach*, which prioritizes predictability and output, moves forward on an efficient and uniform timeline, regardless of the condition of the vine. But *the Flourishing Approach*, as we learned in Chapter 1, is more dynamic. It requires careful observation and a posture of responsiveness rather than control.

Dave continues, "Good vinedressing is relational. We time our cultivation practices in harmony with the vines, the moon cycles, and the seasons."

He then proceeds to explain the ascending and descending cycles of the moon. The gravitational force of these cycles, he tells me, "Pulls upward for two weeks and then pushes downward for two, much like the tides in the ocean or in Lake Michigan. Any surfer will tell you they plan their vacations around those cycles," he adds with a grin. "The earth is about 70% water, but plants are closer to 90%, so the moon phases significantly affect the flow of sap in the vine, and with it, the carbohydrates and nutrients moving through it."

Dave informs me that the moon is currently in a descending phase, which means the energy is being pushed downward into the roots. "This is the time to prune," he says, "because it helps conserve the energy in carbohydrates, amino acids, and everything I want to preserve for bud break. But if I had a really vigorous vineyard, I might choose to prune during the ascending cycle instead, to slow down its growth."

He looks out over the vineyard and continues, "That's where it becomes a relationship. You have to pay attention, to know your vines, and to work with nature instead of against it."

Listening to the Sun and Moon

When Jesus spoke about the vine in John 15, his listeners, immersed in an agricultural world, intuitively understood these rhythms. They knew how to observe the cycles of the seasons. They recognized how nutrients moved with the push and pull rhythm of the moon. These patterns weren't abstract; they were woven into daily life from the very beginning.

In Genesis 1:14, God set the moon and sun in place to "serve as signs to mark the seasons and days and years." Like a giant billboard in the sky, these signs were meant to guide us. They provided a rhythm for life.

The Psalmist writes, "He made the moon to mark the seasons, and the sun knows when to go down."[1] This Psalm is a celebration of how each element of creation faithfully follows this rhythm set by God. Yet, as the *Dictionary of Biblical Imagery* puts it, "one part of God's creation refuses to follow: human beings, confronted with the signs and the testimony, either fall in line and complete the pattern or turn away and break it."[2]

---

1. Psalm 104:19.

2. Leland Ryken, James C. Wilhoit, and Tremper Longman III, eds., *Dictionary of Biblical Imagery* (Downers Grove, IL: InterVarsity Press, 1998), 767.

Like gravity, the sun and moon offer us a "rule of life"—a sacred rhythm we were meant to follow. But in our modern age of technology, air travel, and electricity, we've broken the rules. When the sun goes down, we work on our computers at all hours. We stay up late by fluorescent lights, drive like zombies on highways lit by street lights at 2 a.m., and rise to alarms that override the dawn. We escape winter's chill with tropical vacations and treat the natural aging process as an enemy to resist.

The loving invitation of darkness and dormancy whispers for us to slow down, but it's easily drowned out by the loud mechanical drone of progress. *The Productivity-Driven Approach* drives us to move in opposition to nature's rhythms, especially those that lead us into rest. Yet, ignoring these rhythms comes at a cost. Constant productivity fuels anxiety, burnout, and disconnection from our own souls. When we live as though it is always harvest time, we suffer under the pressure to always be "on." No wonder anxiety is rising.[3] Our souls were never meant to bear the weight of endless harvest.

But Psalm 1:3 reminds us that the righteous person is like a tree planted by streams of water "which yields its fruit *in season*." (*emphasis mine*) Even the healthiest tree does not bear fruit all year long. Like trees, we are not machines that only need a steady stream of electricity or gas to power us to go. For those worn thin by striving for an endless harvest, there is another way. We are living beings, bound to the wisdom of cycles.

---

3. World Health Organization (WHO), *Mental Health Atlas 2017* (Geneva: World Health Organization, 2017), https://www.who.int/publications/i/item/9789241514019?ulm. The WHO recognizes the connection between rising mental health issues such as anxiety and depression and faster work tempos that offer less time for recuperation.

The Cyclical Spiral of Life, Death, and Resurrection

Nature rarely progresses in straight lines. But circles and spirals? It has those in spades. Even the horizon, which appears as a straight line, is in fact a very large sphere. Nothing in creation moves in linear progression. It rises, falls, and rises again in a cyclical rhythm.

This pattern is etched into the very structure of creation; from the earth's tilted rotation that brings us the seasons, to the moon's gravitational pull that gives us the tides, to the turning of the earth toward and away from the sun that gives us day and night. We are not separate from this cycle. We are woven into it daily, monthly, and seasonally, as everything blossoms and withers, dies and rises again.

As the *Dictionary of Biblical Imagery* describes, "Out of nothing came not randomness or chaos, but a divinely ordered progression of time, through segments called seasons, which in themselves show the pattern of life, death, and resurrection."[4]

The Cadence of Jesus' Life

Jesus himself surrendered to this rhythm. Early in his life, he lived in hiddenness and dormancy. We hear no sermons and see no miracles until he is 30. Even then, he intentionally begins his ministry with a prolonged season in the wilderness. There, he descends into the roots of his own soul through silence and solitude, wrestling with Satan in the darkness. Only after emerging from this crucible does he step into his public calling.

From there, his ministry flourishes like branches bursting forth from the vine. The fruit of his life ripens as he proclaims and

---

4. Ryken, Wilhoit, and Longman, *Dictionary of Biblical Imagery*, 767.

embodies the kingdom of God through healings, deliverance, and teaching. The boom of the harvest seems to be everywhere in the Gospels. But, after just three years, the movement of his life descends again, first toward the cross, then into the silence of the grave.

And then, it explodes upwards in resurrection. New life breaks forth like spring buds from barren branches. The resurrection of Christ surges into explosive growth through the early church, ripening into a movement that would bear fruit across generations.

This rhythm of life, death, and resurrection is not just Jesus' story. It's ours. As Paul writes: "For if we have been united with him in a death like his, we will certainly also be united with him in a resurrection like his ... Now if we died with Christ, we believe that we will also live with him."[5]

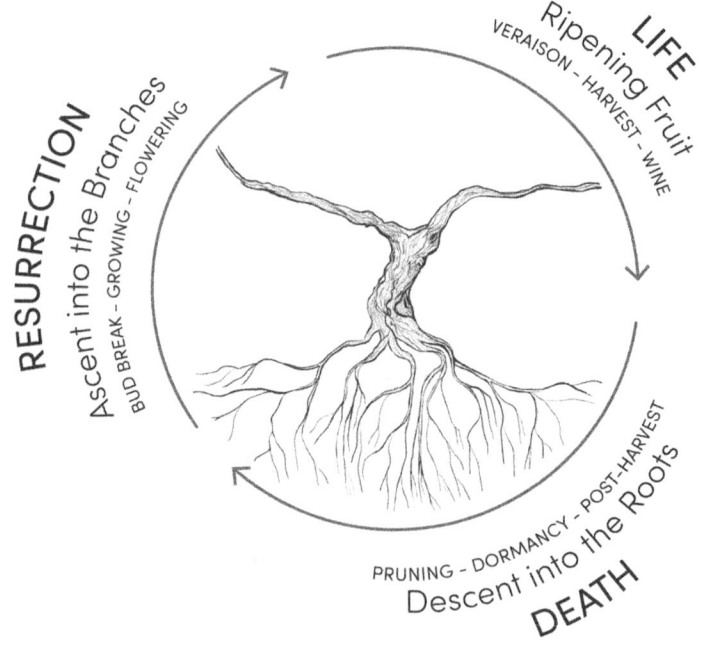

_____

5. Romans 6:5, 8.

The Rhythm is the Plot

If *terroir* is the setting of the story of the vine, and the Vinedresser, Vine, and Branches are the characters, then this rhythm of life, death, and resurrection is the plot. It's the grand story set across the stage of our lives, and even creation remembers it.

One Maundy Thursday, I met Dave in a small vineyard he would soon be pruning. He mentioned that he wouldn't be farming over the weekend.

> Those who study lunar rhythms in agriculture have found that working the land between Good Friday and Easter Sunday negatively affects the plants. The earth remembers the death and resurrection of Christ. For the past 20 years, I've honored this rhythm by resting from farm work over Easter weekend.[6]

Creation itself still feels the repercussions of Jesus going into the tomb. It's as if between Friday and Easter Sunday, it holds vigil in rest and quiet remembrance. But, what about us? How do we live this pattern, especially in the seasons like Christ's death that don't appear productive?

Embracing Rest

During my last staff meeting before I started a six-month sabbatical in February 2020, our small team from West Michigan had gathered around to pray for me. I sat with my hands on my knees, palms facing up as the team encircled my chair. After a long silence, my colleague Dave, who knew me well, spoke:

---

6. Titia Thun and Friedrich Thun, *Maria Thun Biodynamic Calendar: 2025* (City: Publisher, 2024), paperback.

The painting of the pruned vine you did for staff conference came to mind. I feel like there's an opportunity for this sabbatical to be that for you. This sabbatical is going to cut off your ability to work and earn approval from others. Maybe God's not wanting the fruit you bear during sabbatical to be about anything you get done. Maybe he will produce a new kind of fruit in you because you're choosing *not* to work. I know that could be terrifying for you. It could be like living in zero gravity, but I think the fruit is about finding your worth apart from work.

Little did I know how prophetic those words would be. While I entered sabbatical by choice, the world was about to enter its own unchosen one. Just weeks later, the COVID-19 pandemic halted life as we knew it.

During this chaotic time, it was hard not to be anxious. As an achiever who was used to moving toward a goal, I felt restless. Aimless. I often wondered, "Is this rest ok? What should I be doing when the world is turned upside down?"

This forced rest challenged me to take a deeper look at the rest-lessness I felt. I had to consider that perhaps my anxiety about not doing enough had more to do with the expectations I had put on myself from *the Productivity-Driven Approach* rather than from God's expectations of me. Over time, the questions began to change from, *"What should I be doing?"* to *"God, what are you doing in this season?"* and *"How are you shaping me through this?"*

For me, sabbatical allowed the ground to lay fallow so that something new could germinate. But this season of forced rest was not just personal, it was communal. As the world began to shut down and shelter in place, a deeper reckoning emerged: *What was God teaching us when we were forced to stop all the external activity? To wait? To listen? To watch? To pray? How did this season form us collectively like a prolonged dormancy?*

Perhaps the pandemic forced us to let go of the fruit so we could grow a new root system. Beyond the abrupt shift in pace and lifestyle, the pandemic coincided with heightened awareness of systemic racism, sparked by events like the death of George Floyd and the subsequent protests. These moments exposed deep-rooted inequalities that had been growing in the soil for generations. Many of us, especially white Christians like myself, were called into deeper awareness and collective responsibility.

It was a profound season of disruption. But as my friend Danielle Strickland often says, "Disruption is an invitation." Around the world, that upheaval became a shared invitation: to reflect on the impact of injustice, to consider how our collective suffering was shaping us, and to imagine how we might emerge from dormancy with a renewed sense of purpose—one oriented toward the flourishing of all.

What was the Vinedresser tending in you during that season? Perhaps it is only now beginning to bear fruit, or perhaps it won't for many years yet. But, as the *Dictionary of Biblical Imagery* reminds us: "The God who first ordered the seasons of the earth can rightly order the seasons of a human life, bringing each follower of him into maturity, ripeness, and productivity in his own good time."[7]

Rooted in the Rhythm of Death, Life, and Resurrection

The seasons of spiritual growth are rarely uniform. We might experience a full cycle of life, death, and resurrection in a single day. Or, like young vines, we may not see fruit ripen for years.

---

7. Ryken, Wilhoit, and Longman, *Dictionary of Biblical Imagery*, 767.

Some years feel marked by God's silence as we sit for a long time beside Christ in the tomb of loss. But, like the vine, which grows in time with the seasons, we too are invited to live in alignment with this slow, sacred cadence of God's design.

This fall marks my sixth year journeying with these vines through the vibrant seasons of Northern Michigan. I've watched them transform from green to gold, to brown, to barren, and back again.

The Death of Christ: Descending into the Roots

In November, after harvest is over, I've walked through rows of empty vines, their fruit gone, and their brown, papery leaves clinging stubbornly in the wind. With the descending moon cycles and onset of dormancy, the vine's energy sinks into the roots. By January, I've stood alone in the vineyard, feet buried in snow, the silence broken only by the faint scrape of barren branches. Then, in April, the sap rises again, glistening like dew on freshly pruned limbs in the morning sun.

This is the rhythm of Christ's death. Like the vine, we are drawn inward, abiding with Christ in the unseen work beneath the surface.

The Resurrection of Christ: Ascending into the Branches

In May, as the spring dawns and the moon ascends, the vine stirs to life. Energy surges upward into the branches. I've held the fragile buds between my fingers, their felt-like petals unfurling like a hand opening from a fist. Within weeks, the pale sage leaves erupt like geysers, deepening into a lush forest green. By July, I've gently lifted branches full of delicate flowers, their soft green petals brushing against my nose, their warm fragrance like fresh pies from the oven.

This is the rhythm of Christ's resurrection. Our lives rise with him into new expression. Our energy shifts upward as the Vinedresser cultivates our growth in the community of branches.

The Life of Christ: Ripening Fruit

In August, I've tasted lime-green grapes the size of pencil erasers, bursting with a flavor as sharp as Sweet Tarts. The rhythms of descending and ascending work together to mature the fruit. As the earth tilts toward the sun, the clusters swell in the light. By September, I've studied the grapes as they slowly ripen, shifting from bright green to burgundy, one grape at a time. In October, I've sat perched on a white five-gallon bucket, listening to the steady *clip, plunk, clip, plunk* of the grape clusters dropping into another bucket nearby.

This is the rhythm of Christ's life. As we yield our lives for the sake of others, our energy is channeled into the fruit of the kingdom—an offering for the world. It goes into the press so that something new might emerge.

Abiding in Rhythm with Christ

Watching the slow unfolding of each season in the vineyard has reminded me of how my paintings develop. Each color and stroke is unique, revealing something important that needs to be expressed. Yet it's in the layering, the patient, deliberate accumulation over time, that beauty emerges. Full maturity, the moment a piece is ready to be harvested and shared as an offering to the world, may take years. Yet, it's not just the final product that has value—each layer, each season, each vintage offers its own gifts.

This rhythm of the vine has become my own. It has taught me:

To trust the unseen work beneath the surface.

To believe that resurrection always follows death—though rarely on our timeline.

To remember that harvest is fleeting.

And that the fruit is never ours to control, but to offer, trusting God to form something sweet and enduring in its time.

In the chapters ahead, we'll explore how this sacred rhythm—the life, death, and resurrection of Christ—invites us into deep, lasting transformation. Together, we'll learn how to abide with Christ in each season, surrendering to the slow and steady work of the Vinedresser. Each time we move through this cycle, we are formed more fully into the likeness of Christ.

As Richard Rohr writes, "Christ and the soul must die. Christ and the soul must rise. That pattern must happen many times before we understand it."[8]

---

8. Richard Rohr, *The Wisdom Pattern: Order, Disorder, Reorder* (Cincinnati: Franciscan Media, 2020), 68.

Digging Deeper:

1. What might it look like to embrace the rhythm of Christ's life, death, and resurrection in your own life?

2. What habits or cultural pressures tempt you to resist the rhythms of creation, especially the rhythm of rest?

3. Think about how these seasons have shown up in your own life. What are some of the gifts each has offered?

Part II:
The Death of Christ

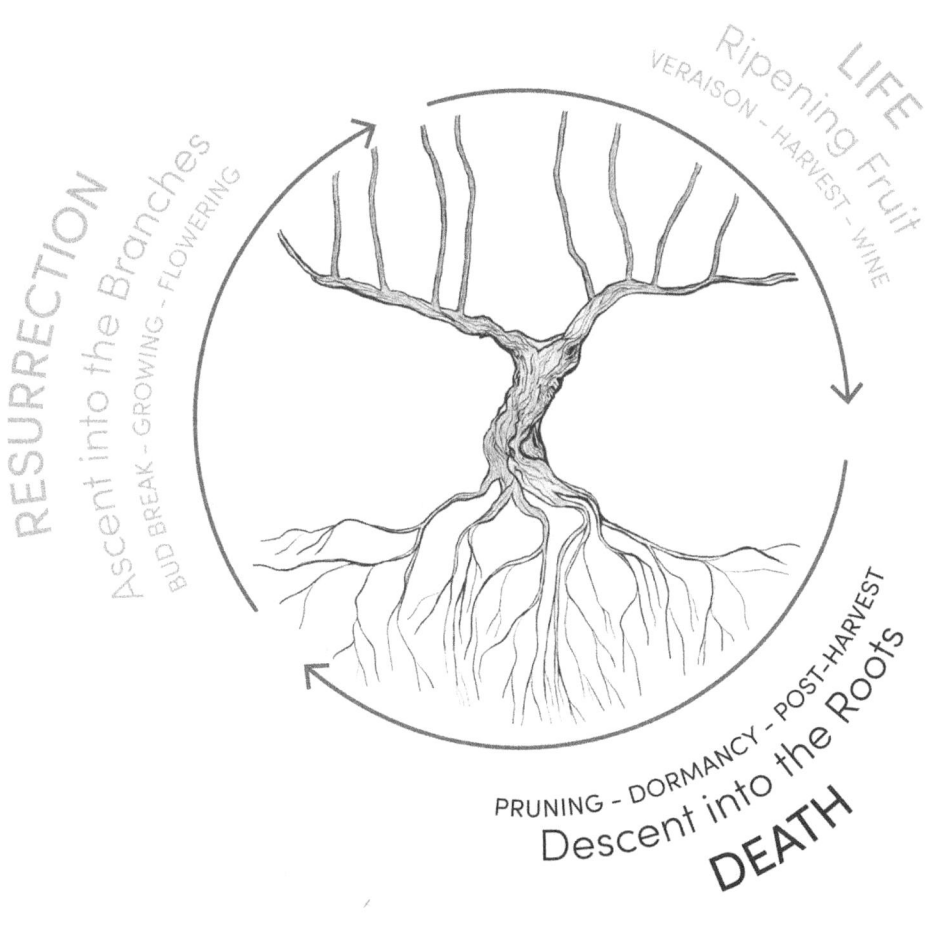

LIFE
Ripening Fruit
VERAISON - HARVEST - WINE

Ascent into the Branches
BUD BREAK - GROWING - FLOWERING
RESURRECTION

PRUNING - DORMANCY - POST-HARVEST
Descent into the Roots
DEATH

Chapter 5:

Descent into the Roots

It is November 11th, a month after the harvest, when I return to Ten Hands Vineyard on Old Mission Peninsula. As I pull onto Happy Hour Lane and catch a glimpse of the vines, I suck in my breath. I hardly recognize them.

What was once a vibrant and lush assortment of greens has cascaded into flickering shades of muted yellow and brown. Just months before, the vines were laden with golden and maroon grapes, but now the leaves sparsely cover the vine, exposing her ribs. The smaller lateral branches have been reduced to short nubs. They poke out like a crown of thorns from the remaining branches, the slender skeletal-like fingers clutching tightly to the wire trellis, holding on for dear life.

Within each row, a few small remaining grape clusters can be found that were missed during harvest. But they look more like raisins, shriveled up and withdrawn inward, shrinking back from the chill of impending winter. Each yellow leaf is cupped upwards to catch a glimpse of the fading sun, and their dry, wafer-thin hands are closing in on themselves in prayer before they are whisked away by the winter winds.

A Shift to the Roots

Dave told me once that at the end of a harvest, after the grapes have been taken to the winery, the leaves absorb the last bits of energy from the waning sun and, in one final push, send it down into the roots, where it will be stored for the winter.

The trajectory of the vine and us in this time is this:

> From life to death
> From light to dark
> From warm to cold
> From outer to inner
> From surface to soil
> From seen to unseen
> The energy descends from the fruits to the roots.

But even as we assess this transition, we are familiar with it, aren't we?

We pass through this phase many times throughout our lives when the sun begins to set in one way or another. We experience the chill of winter when we go through a loss, experience a failure, or come face to face with suffering and death in all kinds of ways.

Sometimes these transitions come upon us slowly. We move from one season of life to another, such as the transition into parenthood or the emergence into adolescence or mid-life. We change careers, shift between projects, or experience a change in leadership.

Other times, these seasons may catch us totally off guard. We encounter the sudden onset of illness, the loss of a loved one, the fallout from a failure, a divorce or breakup, or an unexpected ending in our vocation.

Or maybe, the descent is less visible, but no less real. Perhaps we plunge deep into depression or anxiety. Maybe we come to the end of ourselves in the pattern of addiction.

Whether these seasons come upon us quickly, or slowly descend like the falling of leaves, they are marked by the sensation that something is falling away on one hand, and turning inward on the other. Unlike the natural seasons where we generally expect to experience the resurrection of spring within a few months, these seasons of grief and loss are all-consuming and there is no set timeline for them. When we are in a prolonged period of winter, it's hard to imagine there could ever be a spring.

But, anyone who has experienced loss will tell you that death has a way of clarifying what is important; what has eternal value. All of a sudden, the things that seemed to matter a lot—the unwashed dishes in the sink, the massive work project, the petty conversation with a coworker—start to seem so insignificant and small in light of things like the loss of a loved one or the ending of a marriage.

If you are in one of these seasons, I see you. It's okay to pause here for a moment and simply allow yourself to be in this space, without the pressure to rush toward resurrection. In the coming chapters, we will explore spiritual practices that can help guide us through this dark time mindfully, but be gentle with yourself if you're not ready for that just yet.

It's hard to see how anything good could emerge from seasons of loss. Yet, if we have the courage to face the darkness with God, this is where he does his most transformative work. When losses surround us or stir within us, we are invited to abide with Christ in his death.

As Paul writes in Philippians 3:10–11: "I want to know Christ—yes, to know the power of his resurrection and participation in his sufferings, becoming like him in his death, and so, somehow, attaining to the resurrection from the dead."

The word Paul uses for "participation" in his sufferings is the same as "communion" or "fellowship." Mysteriously, it is through suffering that we experience a unique kind of communion with Christ, one that cannot be known in any other way. And as Paul suggests, the power of Christ's resurrection can only be fully realized when we first abide with him in his suffering. Like the dormancy of winter, this time is considered a vital part of spiritual growth. But it requires us to journey deeply into the heart of our own pain, trusting Christ to meet us there.

Two Types of Dormancy

When vines go dormant, they experience two vital functions: external dormancy (Ecodormancy) and internal dormancy (Endodormancy). External dormancy is what happens on the outside that prevents the bud from breaking, such as soil temperatures declining, while internal dormancy is what happens on the inside of the vine to prepare it for bud break in the next season.

External Dormancy:

Like the sudden arrival of freezing temperatures that trigger dormancy in vines, there are some times in our life when external factors force us to descend into the darkness of the soil. These are the situations that happen *to* us. Like the sudden onset of disease or an unexpected job loss that triggers us to slow down and draw inward, these situations invite us into the deeper, hidden work of the heart. But, these experiences on their own are not what cause growth.

I love what William Bridges says about this in his book, *Transitions: Making Sense of Life's Changes*: "It's not those events [outside us] that make the transition; it's the inner-reorientation and self-re-definition that you have to go through in order to incorporate any of those changes into your life."[1]

In other words, it's not the external changes of the fruit being stripped away or the decrease in temperatures that makes dormancy significant. It's what happens on the *inside* that causes the greatest amount of change. For these transitions to be trans-formative, we must tend to the work God does *within the roots*. According to Terry Walling, in his book, *Stuck! Navigating Life and Leadership Transitions*, in this phase "individuals consolidate past learning, process issues of character, deepen convictions and values, and are prepared for the next phase of their development ... Transitions are more about character development than job description."[2]

---

1. William Bridges, *Transitions: Making Sense of Life's Changes* (Cambridge, MA: Perseus Publishing, 1991), xii.

2. Terry Walling, *Stuck! Navigating Life and Leadership Transitions* (Chico, CA: Leader Breakthru, 2010), 26–27.

Internal Dormancy

During internal dormancy (endodormancy), the vine undergoes essential inner changes that aren't visible on the outside. Inside, metabolic activity slows down, energy is conserved, and the vine builds up tissues to prevent damage from freezing temperatures. During this time, its buds enter a kind of "locked" state. Even when the weather on the outside turns favorable, it won't grow outward.

Like the vine, when we enter this "locked" state, on the surface it seems like nothing is happening. Sometimes it seems that there is a complete halt of activity. But beneath, our souls are doing slow, hidden, and sacred work—often without our awareness.

Walling describes this time as "characterized by a prolonged period of restlessness, self-doubt, lack of motivation, stagnation, diminished confidence, lack of direction, distance from God, isolation, relational conflict and tension, lack of effectiveness, and a struggle to stay focused and motivated."[3]

This kind of experience is similar to what St. John of the Cross, a 16th-century Spanish mystic and poet, described as the "dark night of the soul"[4]—a time of intense spiritual desolation where one experiences a deep sense of inner darkness. It's a dormancy intentionally sought for transformation and deeper union with Christ. It is a time of purification and preparation.

Whether or not this experience is something we seek, as St. John of the Cross describes, or something we simply surrender to, in these dark times, it's hard to see the hand in front of your face, let alone understand why this is happening or what it all means.

---

3. Walling, *Stuck! Navigating Life and Leadership Transitions*, 27.

4. St. John of the Cross, *The Dark Night of the Soul*, trans. E. Allison Peers (New York: Image Books, 1959), 22.

And like the vineyard in the chill of winter, the Vinedresser seems nowhere to be found. It feels as though God has abandoned you, and these seasons are marked by loneliness, despair, spiritual dryness, or even numbness. Yet, it is also a time of spiritual clarification. In this desolate state, we begin to see ourselves and God more acutely and receive more of who God really is.

These internal uprisings are a time to wrestle with the meaning and eternal weight of what God is doing during these times. While in harvest months, we may rightly be preoccupied with the activity and celebration of harvesting, as the leaves turn to beautiful shades of gold and brown, our energy must channel inward and downward like vines in dormancy.

Resistance

In our culture, we tend to resist the pull of descent. It is entirely foreign to the *Productivity-Driven Approach*, where the focus is on fruit bearing. In this perspective, everything must move toward progress, and any sign of decrease in productivity is to be avoided at all costs. But, when we pay more attention to the fruit than the roots, the vine suffers.

The first time Dave and I met, he showed me a small plot of two-year-old vines. Their vibrant green leaves stretched upward, reaching for the top wire of the trellis like a toddler grasping for cookies on a high shelf. "This vine will try to ripen fruit this year," Dave explained, "but I'm going to remove it. Young vines under three years old don't have the root system to grow and bear fruit simultaneously. Before they can sustain fruit, they must anchor deep roots."

Dave then proceeded to tell me a story of a vineyard owner who was in a hurry for his grapes to produce fruit. Lured by an output-driven mindset, he rushed the process. He let two-year-old vines hang grapes before their roots had fully developed. For a year it yielded fruit for harvest, but it burned the vines out. By year four, he could barely get the vines to grow.

When I heard this, I thought of so many ministry leaders I knew who were put under incredible pressure to yield external metrics of growth. They gave most of their time and energy to developing a successful ministry, but when I met with them, their souls were shrinking and shriveling up. Like the parable of the soil in Mark 4, that had no roots, these leaders lacked maturity and could not withstand storms or sweltering heat when they came. They often felt crushed and dehumanized under the weight of expectations and felt used up by a *Productivity-Driven Approach* to ministry. With no attention to their roots, within just a few short years, many of them left ministry work to pursue something else.

This happens in ministry contexts, but it also happens in businesses, hospitals, schools, and all other fields where people are pushed to prioritize outcomes over their own well-being. Without nurturing their inner life and developing resilience through rest, they, too, risk burnout and disillusionment, and the joy is drained from their lives.

But the reality is: a vine's roots are greater in size than the form we see above the surface. What is unseen is what provides the sustenance, stability, and depth for what *is* seen. When we give no attention to the roots, we live lives lacking depth and character. And in the end, this will show itself in the fruit we yield one way or another.

John O'Donohue describes it this way:

> When we devote no time to the inner life, we lose the habit of soul. We become accustomed to keeping things at surface level. The deeper questions about who we are and what we are here for visit us less and less. If we allow time for soul, we will come to sense its dark and luminous depth.

If we fail to acquaint ourselves with soul, we will remain strangers in our own lives.[5]

For deciduous plants, dormancy is critical for life to flourish; they need times of withdrawal, rest, healing, and restoration in order to prepare for the next growing season. As we discussed in the last chapter, God has given us the gift of rest in daily, weekly, and seasonal rhythms: from the setting of the sun, signaling us to cease work and sleep, to the weekly Sabbath, to seasonal rhythms of rest like a vacation or sabbatical.

However, when we have become so indoctrinated and assimilated into the *Productivity-Driven Approach*, we tend to viscerally resist slowing down, resting, and tending to the inner life.

Why? Because when our identity is in the fruit, and it is taken away, we shiver against the cold without it. We face the stark reality of who we are without the fruit. And like the vines exposed after the winter winds have whisked away our leaves, we see the essence of ourselves stripped bare. And for that, we feel a kind of deep shame from which we desperately try to hide.

Sabbatical Dormancy

On one of the first days of my sabbatical, I arrived at a youth camp that, just months earlier, had been alive with the laughter and energy of kids and teenagers. Now, in the stillness of February, it stood quiet and deserted. I had gone there to begin my sabbatical with a silent retreat. I sat in a small room set apart as a place of respite for ministry workers.

---

5. John O'Donohue, *Beauty: The Invisible Embrace* (New York: Harper Perennial, 2004), 39.

I had eagerly prepared with snacks and journals and more books than I could read. I imagined myself like some contemplative, monastic nun receiving endless revelations from God as though I were on the receiving end of some kind of mystical mountain spring. I dreamed that perhaps I would lap it all up with large gulps and come home glowing like Moses coming down from the mountain of Horeb.

Instead, I found myself listless and restless. Cramped in a small room where a bunk bed, rocking chair, and end table filled the small space, I felt walled in and restricted. Too cold to go out and too agitated to sit, I wrestled the chair into a small little nook to look out the window. I fidgeted, trying to get comfortable, but my back ached and I had that irritable feeling you get after having too many sweets.

I tried to be still and calm, but as I sat there with my feet against the windowsill, staring out the window at the trees snapping their branches against one another in the bitter, cold wind, I felt deeply anxious. This nagging and angry sensation started tearing at my insides like a tree that was aggressively stripped of its bark and exposed in the cold.

I tried to find words to pray, but could find none. Instead, I roughly scrawled out several pictures in my sketchbook in some last-ditch effort to make meaning of the emptiness I felt. I drew a sea turtle covered in barnacles so thick you couldn't make out its eyes and mouth. It was lying flat on a table and two large hands were firmly gripping its shell, cutting away the barnacles with a sharp knife. Beneath it, I wrote the words, "aggressively exposed and tender."

I learned later that, as an invasive species, barnacles can grow slowly on turtles over a long period of time. They go largely unnoticed until eventually they take over entirely, keeping the turtle from swimming or eating and weighing it down.

I didn't know how deeply attached I was to my work until I was forced to stop and rest. When work suddenly stopped, I had to come face to face with how many barnacles had covered me.

The ways I had been striving for approval from others.

The sense of validation and purpose I received from my performance.

The way I had kept myself busy to show that I was worth something.

The way I had shapeshifted into who others wanted me to be instead of who I was.

All of these things had collected slowly without my noticing until, eventually, like this sea turtle, I was no longer able to swim freely. I bumbled about with a hard shell, weighed down and crusted over with some grotesque mask that had become a part of me. When all became still and silent in the solitude of winter months, my false self and coping mechanisms were revealed for what they really were: an invasive species that had moved in and taken over.

Sabbatical afforded me the chance to see that these barnacles did not belong to me, but they had dug their jagged little suckers in under the crevices of my shell and would require a lot of painful work to cut loose.

I wasn't prepared for how painful this journey into descent would be. But then again, I didn't realize just how much I had attached my identity to my work. Like a vine that had been clinging to its leaves and grapes as though it needed them to survive, when they were all stripped away, I felt naked.

In the face of exposure, a part of me panicked and lashed out in a desperate attempt to avoid shame. I stayed busy to avoid the direct gaze inward. Because I felt helplessly out of control of what was raging in my insides, I over-compensated by trying to control my outer life. I frantically cleaned the house. I micromanaged my husband. I experienced the kind of deep nothingness Henri Nouwen describes in his book, *The Way of the Heart*:

> In solitude I get rid of my scaffolding: no friends to talk
> with, no telephone calls to make, no meetings to attend,
> no music to entertain, no books to distract, just me—naked,
> vulnerable, weak, sinful, deprived, broken—nothing. It is this
> nothingness I have to face in my solitude, a nothingness
> so dreadful that everything in me wants to go run to my
> distractions so that I can forget my nothingness and make
> myself believe that I am worth something ... Solitude is not
> merely a means to an end. Solitude is its own end. It is the
> place where Christ remodels us in his own image and frees
> us from the victimizing compulsions of the world. Solitude is
> the place of our salvation.[6]

Solitude is one of the vehicles through which God heals us in seasons of dormancy.

When I looked back at the drawing of myself as that turtle covered in barnacles, I looked so helpless. It was clear that there was nothing I could do on my own power to free myself. And in contrast, as I looked at the hands holding onto the turtle, there

---

6. Henri J.M. Nouwen, *The Way of the Heart: Connecting with God Through Prayer, Wisdom, and Silence* (New York: Ballantine Books, 1981), 22.

was a loving intentionality behind them. A purposeful, but careful strength that had the power to cut those barnacles away.

It was as though Jesus came to me in that cabin and, showing me his scars, asked "Do you want to be free?"

As he stood before me, I felt his empathy, compassion, and tenderness toward me. His wounds revealed the very source of healing he offered. The invitation was clear: I could swim away and remain weighed down by those barnacles, or I could lie still and surrender to the Father's loving hands as they firmly, but gently, cut them away. As I experienced his loving gaze upon the grotesque creature I had become—covered in barnacles— instead of experiencing shame, I experienced liberation.

We all need to experience God's loving gaze upon the areas we are stuck in shame. Without it, we can never truly be free. As God beholds us in love, we learn to loosen our grip—on our fig leaves, on our barnacles, on every false attachment.

Detachment from the Fruit

Detachment is the practice of releasing what we cling to for identity or fulfillment and turning instead toward the true source of life: the Vine. These times remind us that our identity is not found in the fruit we bear, but in our connection to the Vine itself. After the harvest, a branch doesn't cease to be a branch simply because it no longer bears fruit. Even in darkness and dormancy, it remains part of the vine.

St. John of the Cross saw the dark night of the soul as an essential path toward spiritual maturity and intimacy with God. When our earthly attachments and self-reliance are stripped away, we are drawn into greater union with Christ. Like vines surrendering their leaves to winter dormancy, this is a season of relinquishment—letting go of what is external so we can receive the hidden life that flows from the roots.

In the depths of the soil, we come to understand our belovedness in God apart from our fruit. We encounter his loving gaze upon us even in our failures, mistakes, and shame. As we let go of our tight grip on the coverings of our false selves—our performance, our addictions, our status—we see that we are still grafted into Christ. And that is the truest thing about us. From that deeply rooted place in Christ, we grow into our truest selves and rise with new life when spring comes.

Like the vine that retreats into silence and stillness during winter, the journey of descent into our roots leads us there, too. We follow Jesus who went there first and shows us the way.

And the way is surrender.

The Posture of Surrender: Christ's Descent into the Roots

At the end of his life, when Jesus descended into a season of dormancy in his death, the text says he then "bowed his head and gave up his spirit." This word for "gave up," *paradidomi*, means to surrender, to yield, to deliver oneself into the hands of another."[7]

Rather than fighting or running from the path of descent, Jesus surrendered to it.

---

7. Larry Pierce, *Outline of Biblical Usage*, s.v. "παραδίδωμι (paradidōmi, G3860)," Blue Letter Bible, accessed January 12, 2024, https://www.blueletterbible.org.

When Jesus surrendered his life, he didn't just surrender *something*, he surrendered *to someone*—to the loving arms of the Father—as he yielded to death. As David Benner writes in *Surrender to Love: Discovering the Heart of Christian Spirituality*:

> Surrender involves too much vulnerability to be a responsible action in relation to anything other than unconditional love. Ultimately, of course, this means that absolute surrender can only be offered to Perfect Love. Only God deserves absolute surrender, because only God can offer absolutely dependable love.[8]

Why did Jesus surrender in descent? Because he trusted the One to whom he surrendered —the Vinedresser who knows that going down into the roots is what brings forth bud break and new life, not only for Christ but for all creation.

Choosing to Stay in Dormancy

Here, in Northern Michigan, dormancy extends from November to May. That's half the year where there is no visible sign of growth. There are regulators inside the buds of vines that keep them from growing before their time.

But most of us have lost touch with this internal regulator in our souls. We frequently rush through seasons of descent as though it will pass quickly, like a cold, if we just give ourselves a day or two of rest. But sooner or later, we come to the hard realization that seasons like these often carry on longer than we would like.

This was especially evident during the COVID-19 pandemic. Andy Crouch, Kurt Keilhacker, and Dave Blanchard observed in

---

8. David G. Benner, *Surrender to Love: Discovering the Heart of Christian Spirituality* (Downers Grove, IL: InterVarsity Press, 2003), 61–62.

their *Praxis Journal* article that many of us expected the crisis to blow over like a winter storm. But it ended up dragging on like an ice-age, altering us and our world in irreversible ways.[9]

If we want to experience the transformation God has to offer in the roots of the inner life, we must *choose* to stay in the darkness of the soil, for however long it takes, with a level of expectancy for what it will produce in us.

Dormancy is not just a season of waiting for spring to return—it's that something necessary is happening in the waiting. As Rich Villodas says, "what God does in us as we wait is often much more important than what we are waiting for."[10] In seasons of grief, transition, or spiritual disorientation, God strengthens our root system and prepares us for growth that isn't yet visible. It is deep soul work that cultivates us to be ready for resurrection life. We must choose to remain there and allow God to finish his work as he grows us in character, perseverance, and our identity in him.

While the harvest is still a long way off, we have to trust that this is the work God has called us to do now—the inner work, the hidden work that no one else sees—and trust that this work, in time, will one day yield a harvest worth gathering.

9. Andy Crouch, Kurt Keilhacker, and Dave Blanchard, "Leading Beyond the Blizzard: Why Every Organization Is Now a Startup," *The Praxis Journal*, Praxis, March 20, 2020, https://journal.praxislabs.org/leading-beyond-the-blizzard-why-every-organization-is-now-a-startup-b7f32fb278ff.

10. Rich Villodas (@richvillodas), Instagram post, December 5, 2023, https://www.instagram.com/p/C02j04dgmBr/.

Digging Deeper:

1. Can you recall a season that led you to turn inward, slow down, and wait? What resistance did you face?

2. How might a season of loss or waiting be an invitation to commune with Christ in his suffering? In what ways does this differ from what you've been taught?

3. In what ways have you tied your identity to the "fruit" of what you produce? How might God be inviting you to embrace a season of detachment?

Chapter 6:

Post-Harvest

One frigid day in November, I spot Tom, the owner of Ten Hands Vineyard, in the small valley between the Riesling and Chardonnay vines, hard at work with his buddy (also named Tom) who owns a neighboring vineyard down the road. They are shoveling thick clumps of dirt into a compost pile enclosed in a cylindrical wire fence.

Surrounding them are piles of manure, grass clippings, and leaves. Nearby is a rusted metal trash can full of burned pruning clippings. Tom tells me that when the pruning clippings are burned, they emit carbon that promotes the growth of fungi which aids decomposition and helps the roots access nutrients more efficiently.

Next to the trash can, I am a bit shocked to see that a part of the compost is the head of a small 7-point deer buck from Tom's hunting expedition that fall. It rests gently in the middle of an abandoned car tire on the grass.

Just a few feet from the compost brew is a cylindrical stack of pressed grapes that look like an abandoned birthday cake on the lawn. The cake is made out of the remains of the previous harvest's pressings for Tom's personal batch of wine. The bottom layer is the deep burgundy of Merlot and Blaufränkisch grapes, while the top layer makes up the golden brown skins of Chardonnay, Pinot Blanc, and Riesling. Tom and Tom are working all of these items together to form some kind of compost gumbo that will stew over winter and be ready to spread over the roots of the vines in the spring.

Composting

Dave told me once, "When vinedressers pick grapes off their vines, they are taking the most important part of the plant, so they must be intentional to add nutrients back into the soil to replenish the roots through composting."

The elements of the past season are all incorporated together to nourish the vine for the next. Nothing is wasted. Everything cast aside will be used to feed a community of microbes hidden to the naked eye. The cyclical rhythm of their life, death, and excretion in the soil provides the sustenance that nourishes the roots.

This unseen process beneath the soil is like the hidden work in our own lives. After a harvest, we, too, need replenishing. God intentionally adds nutrients back into the soil of our souls to replenish us.

Feet covered in dirt, God invites us to take an honest look with him at the remains of our past triumphs and failures. He collects them and, together, we work them into the soil to nourish the roots of who we are becoming.

We collect the shriveled grape skins—both the gifts of the harvest and the remains of its pressed fruit. We carefully observe the thin wrinkles of wisdom they carry and gently fold them into the compost pile.

We collect the dead leaves and grass clippings that have soaked up the life and warmth of the sun—the wisdom from books, mentors, diverse voices, inspiring moments, and times in prayer. We take the nutrients from these sources and meditate on them more deeply now, letting them sink into the soil to nourish us as we withdraw.

We observe the articles of death and decay—the memories of what has died that call for our attention. Perhaps we take in the remembrance of loved ones we have lost and mindfully hold them close for a time. And with the sting of loss in our chest, we heave their memories into the pile, intentionally folding them into the soil.

We take what was once pruned away—the dry sticks of past rejections, opportunities, and commitments that had been pain-fully cut back in order to channel growth somewhere else. With a sigh, we heave them into the metal trash bin and let them burn, the carbon coalescing into charred remains. And then, in large shovelfuls, we toss them into the compost heap, too.

And lastly, we fold into the mix the most important ingredient: manure. As Dave says, "Manure is the best and fastest way to change the quality of the soil." There is no sugarcoating this. What was once waste—the stinky, debased, undignified, and flat-out nasty parts of our stories—is transformed into the nutrients we need to grow.

Confession

In post-harvest descent, we face the parts of ourselves that look and smell like manure. Our mistakes. Our failures. The inner demons that come to the surface during these times. It is painful to have these parts of ourselves exposed; yet, this is the start of becoming free.

This is what it means to participate with Christ in his death. To bring to him all the ways we have felt the sting of sin and death and allow his healing work of the cross to transform it all. Here, after the harvest, we must bring all of these things into the light of God's presence, like a giant heap of compost gumbo that gets worked into the soil to grow something new. This is the work of confession.

At its core, confession is telling the truth. The truth about what happened to us. The truth about what we have done to others. The truth about the grave injustices and pain surrounding us, and the stories we create to make sense of them. The truth about the lies we have believed that have shaped our stories.

When we go through traumatic, painful, or even just stressful circumstances, we often form stories from gut and knee-jerk responses to anxiety, shame, and stress. We tend to make snap judgments about the real threat. And when we do this, we create a false narrative based on an oversimplified view of ourselves, others, and our world.

In confession, we name the story we are telling ourselves in our pain. Anne Lamott describes this as the s****y first draft.[1] This is where we let out our inner five-year-old that throws tantrums and dramatizes everything. The one who cries out in pain and anger and frustration at what is happening. Some of what we cry out is based in truth, some not. Here, we tend to make polarized statements about who is the villain and who is the victim. Usually, we are the victim—whether or not this is accurate.

In confession, our unchecked emotions come to the surface in the safety of a loving God who is strong enough to handle our rage and skewed perceptions of reality.

In that safe space, we encounter parts of ourselves that have been shaped by pain, stifled, or denied that start emerging from the dark caverns within us. They may clamor for immediate relief, making demands for a quick fix of coffee, a sweet treat, a glass of wine, or venting to a friend. But the solution isn't to simply satisfy their demands.

Instead, these parts need time, attention, and the safety of being seen. When we meet them with curiosity and compassion, we can give them a name and listen to their deeper needs, trusting that each part has something important to tell us, even if their strategies are misguided. When we ask them what they truly long for, we begin to heal. As their needs are met, they no longer have to act out in ways that sabotage us.[2]

We must do this work, as crazy and hairy as it is, because whether or not we name these stories, we will act them out. We will live

---

1. Anne Lamott, *Bird by Bird: Some Instructions on Writing and Life* (New York: Anchor Books, 1995), 21.

2. This kind of work is at the heart of Internal Family Systems (IFS), a therapeutic framework that sees the self as made up of various "parts." See more in Glossary.

from a false narrative and just roll through life in this self-protecting, survival mode that shields us from others and from God. In confession, we dig deep into the soil to assess what is really driving us.

We are invited to ask questions like:

- Why am I pushing myself so hard? What's underneath the striving?

- Why do I scroll Instagram endlessly?

- Why do I keep checking my email?

- Why do I get so defensive when someone critiques me?

- What's behind my impulse to leave the room when someone brings up the past?

When we learn to get curious about the fruit of our actions and work our way backwards, down through the trunk of our thoughts and feelings, we can sort through the compost to find out what is feeding the roots of our desires and motives.

For compost to transform into something that is rich in nutrients that feed the roots, it needs to be exposed to oxygen and light. In confession, we dig through the layers of guilt and shame to get to the truth. We bring forth the decaying, smelly, and ugly parts of our past into the light of Christ. As we do, as Paul writes, "everything exposed by the light becomes visible—and everything that is illuminated becomes a light."[3]

In the light of Christ's presence, we begin to see ourselves and our situation from God's perspective: how he feels about what happened, and the painful reality of where we have contributed to the way things are. And there, we must lament the truth.

---

3. Ephesians 5:13.

Lament

Lament is an active surrender to God in grief and sorrow. It is where we courageously face the darkness and say "this isn't the way it was supposed to be. This is ugly and broken and wrong. But Jesus is here in the midst of it, and I will turn to him."

In lament, we speak honestly with God about the wounds we carry—our own and those of others. We count the cost of sin and the devastation it has caused. And in that honesty, we are invited to move from worldly sorrow, which leads to death, into godly sorrow.

Worldly sorrow is rooted in self-pity, self-justification, bitterness, or in attempts to numb the pain of guilt through self-medicating. This kind of sorrow traps us in cycles of despair and ultimately leads to death.

In contrast, godly sorrow opens the door to transformation. Paul describes it this way in 2 Corinthians 7:10, "Godly sorrow brings repentance that leads to salvation and leaves no regrets." It produces an eagerness to make things right, a longing to change, and a readiness to pursue justice.[4]

Lament reorients us to God. It loosens our death grip on the false messiahs we cling to for rescue from pain—our achievements, relationships, politics, even our ministry. In lament, we release these empty attachments and instead surrender instead to Jesus, Emmanuel (God with us) in the darkness. As we turn to him in our mourning, grieving what has been lost, we receive the blessing Jesus promises in the Beatitudes, "Blessed are those who mourn, for they will be comforted."[5]

---

4. 2 Corinthians 7:11.

5. Matthew 5:4.

Here, in the tomb of our grief, we make space for the Divine Comforter to meet us with tender compassion. As we abide with Christ in his death, we participate in godly sorrow, grieving the sin that put him on the cross. And there, in his presence, he transfigures our wounds into glory.

Transfiguring Our Wounds

"Allowing our always unjust wounds to, in fact, become sacred wounds, is the unique Christian name for salvation."[6]

- Richard Rohr

When we take the posture of Christ and surrender to God at the cross through lament, a powerful exchange occurs. He takes our wounds upon himself and transfigures them. Like the vine that sucks up the compost from the soil and transforms it into sap that nourishes the vine, Christ takes the smattering piles of our compost and transfigures them into kingdom fruit.

> At the cross, he transfigures our shame into glory.
>
> He transfigures rejection into belonging.
>
> He transfigures unworthiness into purpose.
>
> He transfigures suffering into joy.
>
> He transfigures hate into love.
>
> He transfigures lies into truth.

---

6. Richard Rohr, *The Wisdom Pattern: Order, Disorder, Reorder* (Cincinnati, OH: Franciscan Media, 2020).

The manure meant to humiliate us is transfigured into fertilizer that nourishes us into the image of Christ. As this exchange takes place, we begin to see our lives with eternal perspective.

As I mentioned in Chapter 3, for me, this journey began at *the Beauty and the Formation of the Soul Retreat* when God started to liberate my true artist self. During my sabbatical, in solitude and silence, I was forced to detach from the false, chameleon-like self that had been shapeshifting into whatever people wanted me to be in order to belong.

The next step required me to go back into the roots to uncover where this false identity started showing up. If shapeshifting (transforming myself to be who others wanted me to be) was the fruit, then what were the roots? When did I start to believe that my artist self didn't belong? When did I start shapeshifting into someone else?

God brought me back to a moment on my first day of class at seminary. Our professor had us go around the room and share what our major was in undergrad. One by one, I watched my peers say, "Bible major, Theology major, Bible major, Theology major, Theology major, Christian Leadership, Christian Education, Bible major."

As I scanned the room of mostly men and heard their answers, I nervously shifted in my chair. Did I miss the memo on Christian college? When it came my turn and I said, "Art major," I already wanted to hide under my desk.

My professor smiled as if to reassure me and asked enthusiastically, "Oh! You know what great theologian was an artist!?"

My heart lilted with excitement as I asked, "Who?" but he chuckled to himself as if answering a joke and said, "Oh, no one."

Color rushed to my cheeks and there was nowhere to hide. I felt exposed, naked, and ashamed. Desperate to appear occupied, I dropped my gaze to the syllabus, skimming the pages of class expectations: the lengthy reading lists, the professional dress code, and the high academic standards.

At 22 years old, I was quickly losing my way, grasping for something to hold on to, something to buoy me up and keep me afloat. A series of thoughts came flooding in rapid succession, and I grabbed ahold of them as if they could save me:

> Maybe I can prove that I belong here ...
> Maybe if I show up on time and dress professionally and work really hard and get straight As and preach the best sermons and be really articulate in class ...
> Maybe if I don't ask too many questions or challenge the status quo ...
> Maybe if I can do exactly what my professors are asking of me and nail it on every exam ...
> Maybe if I can give all the right answers and could just blend in and be like everyone else ...
> they would see that women can lead and teach ...
> They will see that even artists can do this too ...
> and then I would belong.

The next day, I picked out a black outfit. I wore makeup and straightened my hair like a line. I worked a part-time job and took a full load of classes. I poured myself into my studies and worked particularly hard on my sermons. But I stopped painting.

I colored within the lines of the academic environment I was in. In order to succeed, I had to think rational thoughts and give rational answers. I had to write critical papers like my professors told me to and shut down my emotions because I was told they couldn't be trusted when approaching the text.

And over three long years, the color within me faded. I became an empty shell of myself. On the outside, I was nailing it with straight As and accolades. I even earned a preaching award from my complementarian professor. But on the inside, I was dying. That fiery, audacious, bold, sensitive, and creative artist was long gone. There was no room for her there.

My guess is we all have stories like this. Stories where we receive a message, intended or unintended, that we don't belong. That we are not loved and accepted for who we are. Maybe it was in kindergarten or maybe in middle school. Maybe it was in college. Maybe some of us are still living in that story today. The story that says we cannot show the world who we are, because if we do, we will be rejected. So we hide our true selves away.

But, this is why we need to tend to our roots. Because Jesus is not content to leave us bound in that kind of shame. He wants to set us free.

Years after that moment in seminary, Jesus invited me back to the memory through inner-healing prayer with a trained prayer minister. When I went back into that room in my mind, and I felt my face flush with shame at my professor's words all over again, I saw myself sitting there, the sole woman artist in a room of men, and I felt desperately alone.

But, when the woman guiding me in prayer asked, "What does Jesus want you to see?" Something strange happened. When I looked a second time, I saw myself with giant wings. Have you ever seen the X-men movie with the character Angel? The one who has large wings draping behind him along the ground beneath his trench coat? That's how big they were. And they were taking up so much space that no one could sit next to me.

Jesus said, "Bette, these wings are the prophetic artist gift I've given you. You are my divine messenger. I have created you to fly up and see from my perspective, and then you are to come down and deliver that word through what you write, what you speak, and what you paint. Wings don't belong in a classroom. You were made to fly."

It's hard to explain what happened when I saw that picture and heard those words from Jesus. It continues to be one of the most powerful and liberating things I've ever seen and heard. Somehow, Jesus took one of the most painful, wounding experiences of my life and turned it into one of the most beautiful memories I have with him in prayer. He transfigured my wounds of rejection into eternal belonging. He gave me an image of my divine identity that I continue to come back to over and over again when I need to be reminded of who I am: his divine messenger.

Repentance

The word *repentance* means "to turn aside," it is a call to live differently in response to the truth. For me, repentance has meant turning away from the false, wounded self and learning to live from my healed, true self—empowered by the Spirit. But this transformation doesn't happen all at once.

When we suffer a loss, go through rejection, or experience the sting of death, the wounds we have accumulated run deep. Sometimes, long after we think we've moved on, the same pain point gets retriggered. We suffer another loss, another failure, or another rejection that awakens the same old lie the enemy has used to keep us bound. But what if, in those very moments, God is not abandoning us—but inviting us to heal more deeply?

The brain is a complex network of neural pathways. When we experience trauma—especially repeated trauma—it carves grooves into our patterns of response. Instinctively, we return to those well-worn paths. Healing requires intentional practice: choosing different responses, again and again, and repeatedly receiving God's loving truth and compassion into those same wounded places. Over time, this creates new neural pathways that lead toward freedom.

God leads us through this cycle of confession–lament–repentance many times over throughout our lives because God intends to redeem it all. There is no nook of your thoughts, no shadowed cranny of the world where the light of his liberating presence doesn't long to heal and restore.

Only Jesus can transfigure wounds into glory—but he invites our participation. This holy work calls us to slow down and do the deep work of uncovering pain, bringing it into the light, and allowing God to transform it into something new. Each time through the cycle, he leads us deeper into restoration—turning unjust wounds into sacred wounds, and composting pain into nourishment for our roots.

Yet this work is not done in isolation. While we may need to withdraw into solitude for part of the process, full healing happens in the context of community. As Dr. Curt Thompson says, "healing takes place when we tell our stories as truly as we can tell them in the presence of an empathetic listener."[7] When we risk bringing our shame into the light of loving presence, we create space for compassion—and a new story begins to emerge.

The Work of the Kingdom in Post-Harvest

The great lie of *the Productivity-Driven Approach*, of course, is that to stop, to confess, to lament, to forgive, and to work through healing isn't worthwhile because it doesn't contribute to our bottom line. Since we aren't being visibly "productive" during

---

7. Dr. Curt Thompson, remarks from the retreat *Beauty and the Formation of the Soul* at the Hermitage (Three Rivers, MI, 2019), used with permission.

these times, the process of descending into our roots is often rushed or avoided altogether in favor of maintaining "business as usual."

But the truth is that this deep work of confession, lament, and repentance *is* the work of the kingdom. Literally, the work of the kingdom is to participate in Christ's reconciliation—the One who is "reconciling to himself all things,"[8] including every part of us that has been fragmented and exiled. Only by engaging in the hard, uncomfortable, and often painful inner work of reconciliation—with God, ourselves, and others—can we hope to bear fruit that looks like the kingdom of God.

Digging Deeper:

1. As you reflect on your own "compost pile" of experiences, what is one area you sense God inviting you to bring into his light to allow him to heal and transform?

2. What false narratives have you been telling yourself about a painful experience, and how might confession help bring clarity and healing?

---

8. Colossians 1:20.

For those navigating trauma, stress, or seasons of descent, here are a few guideposts to begin the journey:

1. **Work with a trauma-informed therapist.** Seek a licensed professional (consider working with a trained Internal Family Systems practitioner) who understands how trauma affects the body and soul.

2. **Practice confession.** In prayer or with a trusted spiritual director, name the truth of your story before God. Write your "s*****y first draft" by allowing the unfiltered version of your story to surface in God's light.

3. **Practice lament.** Don't skip the grief. Mourning is the way to comfort and healing.

4. **Stay rooted in community.** Find people who can sit with you in the dark, without rushing you toward the light, and listen to your story with empathy.

5. **Transfigure your wounds through inner-healing prayer.** In a safe environment with trained facilitators, in prayer, consider revisiting memories where you were wounded. Ask God to show you what lies you received there that have shaped your identity. Look for Jesus. What does he want to show you? What truth does he want to speak over you to replace the lies?

6. **Repent.** How is God inviting you to live differently in light of the truth?

Remember, healing isn't linear. May the composting process unfold slowly and allow God to take the things you wanted to discard and transfigure them into nutrients for your growth.

Chapter 7:

Dormancy

The drive out to Old Mission Peninsula is slow and silent. On my way to take photos of the vines in dormancy at Ten Hands Vineyard this frigid January morning, I am caught behind a snowplow slowly pushing its way along the edges of the road. Normally, I'd drive around, but not today.

Today, the second coldest day of the year—a mere 16 degrees Fahrenheit, or -8.9 degrees Celsius—is a day for slowness, stillness, and paying attention. As the snowplow groans past, I catch fleeting glimpses of East Grand Traverse Bay. The sharp scrape of metal on asphalt startles a flock of ducks into flight, their wings skimming over sea-glass blue water laced with a thin layer of ice.

A fog has descended over the bay, so that I can just barely make out Elk Rapids where Dave's wine garden rests on the other side. The vineyards start appearing in long rows of sprawling vines descending toward the bay in the snow; the wooden trellis posts form dotted lines along the hills like tall narrow tombstones. Between them, the vines throw up their bare arms toward the sky. Their barren branches look so thin and fragile, I wonder how they have the strength to hold the weight of leaves and grapes in the summer months.

As I turn onto Happy Hour Lane, I get a closer look at the vines that no longer carry the remains of dead leaves. The branches stand erect and tall, connected together in an act of solidarity amidst the cold. The burnt sienna branches stand in sharp contrast to the white snow. All that remains is the bony structure of the vine.

After an intense snowstorm and blowing winds, the snow has collected in soft ridges like a miniature mountain range. On most summer days, I would wander the vineyards for hours, taking photos. Today, I can only stand the cold for a few moments before I need to return to my car and get warm. But the vines don't seem to mind. Their branches gently bend toward one another in a frozen dance, immobilized by the wire trellis, their fingertips moving ever so slightly toward one another as if to say hello.

In the open valley between two rows of vines is the cylindrical container of the compost gumbo Tom and Tom whipped up in November—now covered in a tarp. Surrounding it are the abandoned tools left to rest. The yellow-handled shovel and rake lean against the wire cage, and a wheelbarrow is tipped upside down against a snowbank, forgotten at the end of a long workday.

I text Dave: "Is there anything interesting happening in the wine-making or vinedressing process that I should see?"

He replies: "Everything is pretty quiet right now. The wines are resting and vines are dormant."

When I have asked vinedressers to tell me about what is going on during dormancy, they often have a hard time answering my question. Dormancy embraces unseen mysteries hidden to the naked eye.

In dormant seasons in our own lives, we may find ourselves anxious when it seems like nothing is happening. We are often asking, "when will this be over?" or "what do I do next?" Here, we feel the great silence of God most severely. In winter, the Vinedresser is seemingly absent from the scene. What *is* God doing in these seasons after all? But like the vines, the essential work is happening beneath the surface.

Just as gardening tools are set aside during winter, we, too, must set aside the tools we used during growing and harvest. As we let go of our death grip on control, our hands open to receive the gifts God offers us in this season.

The Gift of Rest

Vines essentially go to sleep during dormancy, conserving energy for the season to come. In the same way, rest allows us to replenish what's been depleted. We are restored physically, mentally, and spiritually, so we can face future challenges with renewed clarity and strength.

Our souls need rest just as much as our bodies. Each day, we encounter countless small stressors and emotional weights that accumulate over time:

- The side-eye from your boss during a presentation

- The curt comment from your roommate as they walked out the door

- The unreturned phone call from a friend

- ❧ The pressure to prepare for back-to-back meetings in the cracks between

- ❧ The conversation when you listened intently to the burden of a friend

- ❧ The unresolved grief that keeps showing up unexpectedly

- ❧ The ongoing acts of trauma and injustice toward others or ourselves

All these things take a toll on our souls daily and they add up over time. If we don't take the time for soul-rest, we can become like what happens to us when we miss sleep: walking zombies that are unable to offer our best selves. In rest, we can slow down and allow God the space to heal and restore our souls, giving us the nourishment, strength, and endurance to face future challenges we cannot yet see.

In dormancy, we not only receive the gift of rest, but we are opened up to receive another most unexpected gift: the gift of play.

The Gift of Play

Brené Brown describes play as "anything that makes us lose track of time and self-consciousness, creating the clearing where ideas are born."[1] In essence, play allows our brains to rest and reset in order to spark creativity. What we often perceive as a waste of time in *the Productivity-Driven Approach* is actually a way God hard-wired our brain to become generative with

---

1. Brené Brown, *The Gifts of Imperfection: Let Go of Who You Think You're Supposed to Be and Embrace Who You Are* (Center City, MN: Hazelden, 2010), 100.

innovation. In play, the inner child that is often locked behind the bars of social approval is set free to simply be fully present and create out of her true self.

During my sabbatical, God gently led me to confront my resistance to play. As an achiever who tends to see play as a waste of time, one resource that helped me was *The Artist's Way: A Spiritual Path to Higher Creativity*, by Julia Cameron. In it, we were encouraged to identify our inner Censor, the voice that sabotages play and creativity.[2] After several days of reflection, I woke up with a vivid image of mine: the evil stepmother from Disney's *Cinderella*, the animated version. You know, the one with the big, gray hair shaped like a heart?

All my true self wanted was to put on that dress and dance with Jesus at the ball—to swirl unhindered and free in his presence in a spontaneous dance of play in the creative process. But the evil stepmother inside of me waved the keys to creative freedom with conditional love: *"If you finish your chores, then you can go to the ball. You can create, but only after the real work of ministry is done."*

The perspective of Internal Family Systems Therapy[3] helped me recognize this character as a part of me, an internal manager, who believed that strict control, discipline, and duty were the only way to stay safe and accepted.

And so, there was no room for play. I became the dutiful daughter. The responsible leader. The faithful friend. The one people could count on.

---

2. Julia Cameron, *The Artist's Way: A Spiritual Path to Higher Creativity* (TarcherPerigee, 1992), 34.

3. Richard C. Schwartz, *Internal Family Systems Therapy*, 2nd ed. (New York: Guilford Press, 2019).

Julia Cameron describes this way of thinking as the virtue trap:

> Many people, caught in the virtue trap, do not appear to be self-destructive to the casual eye. Bent on being good husbands, fathers, mothers, wives, teachers, whatevers, they have constructed a false self that looks good to the world and meets with a lot of worldly approval. ... Virtuous to a fault, these trapped creatives have destroyed the true self, the self that didn't meet with much approval as a child. The self who heard repeatedly, "Don't be selfish!" But, the true self is a disturbing character, healthy and occasionally anarchistic, who knows how to play.[4]

I was trapped by the lie of the evil stepmother—the part of me that insisted *work must come before play*. I pushed myself to exhaustion, always promising that when the list was done, then I could finally go to the ball with Jesus and create. But as the mouse, Jaq Jaq, says in the film, "She'll never get to the ball. You'll see. They'll make sure of it. Work, work, work, morning, noon and night."

It didn't matter how many to-do lists I achieved. It was never enough. This part would always move the goalposts. I saw in it the tactics of the evil one: to keep me trapped in my false self under the tyranny of *the Productivity-Driven Approach*. He never intended to free me.

But one day, as I watched Cinderella go to the ball anyway and dance with her prince, I saw something I longed for. In my journal, I wrote, *"Her gaze is completely transfixed on the prince who has captured her full attention. In full display of them all, they are dancing in a trance and captivated in wonder of each other as the others watch in awe. And that's how I want my life and ministry to be—a continual, beautiful dance with Jesus that causes others to look on in wonder."*

---

4. Cameron, *The Artist's Way*, 99.

It took repeated immersions into play, in the hidden place of the studio and on the page, for my creativity to be liberated. As I danced with Jesus in that quiet, sacred space, I began to collaborate with God in ways that were life-giving and free. As I did, I began to receive his creative inspiration and eternal dreams.

The Gift of Dreams

As plants go dormant, they enter a kind of sleep: a mysterious communion with the unseen world of the soil. In much the same way, when we sleep, we tap into the mystery of a world beyond words. Dreaming opens the door to imagination and creative problem-solving. In this state, the logical left brain steps aside, and the brain as a whole becomes more active. Studies using functional MRI scans show that during the dreaming phase in REM sleep, the brain lights up with activity, especially in regions tied to emotion, memory, and creativity.[5] In this space, buried ideas and subconscious memories rise to the surface, forming new insights and those unexpected "eureka" moments. The imagination awakens to divine possibility.

Some of history's greatest innovators knew this and intentionally made space for the liminal state between sleep and waking to receive creative insight. Salvador Dalí, Albert Einstein, and Aristotle all placed themselves in a half-dream state to capture ideas. Beethoven would reportedly nap in his carriage to receive melodies. Thomas Edison held steel balls in his hands as he dozed off, so the crash when they dropped would wake him just as inspiration struck. These innovators discovered what many

---

5. Pierre Maquet et al., "Functional Neuroanatomy of Human Rapid-Eye-Movement Sleep and Dreaming," *Nature* 383, no. 6596 (1996): 163–166, https://doi.org/10.1038/383163a0.

mystics and creatives have long known: the space between dreaming and waking is a thin place.

> It's a space between the conscious and unconscious.
> Between the transcendent and immanent.
> Between heaven and earth.

This is the space of inspiration. Here, we are most ready to encounter the eternal. Our guard is down, so to speak, and God can speak to us more acutely. When we surrender control in our bodies and minds, our souls awaken.

Tim Mackie, co-creator of The Bible Project, put it this way in a talk at the 24-7 Prayer Conference:

> It is in states of serene surrender and vulnerability, especially during sleep, that we are most in touch with reality as it really is. Those are precisely the moments where we have the potential to encounter the person who is paradise, the person of Jesus.[6]

Is it any wonder, then, that God speaks so often through dreams in Scripture? These dreams didn't come through human effort or accomplishment. They were given as a gift while the dreamers were resting—unaware, but receptive. In a state of total surrender, they received glimpses into heavenly reality—the true reality undergirding all things.

Consider the story in Daniel 2. Faced with an impossible task—interpreting King Nebuchadnezzar's dream without even hearing it—Daniel responds not with striving, but with prayerful dependence. During the night, God reveals the mystery in a vision. The

---

6. Tim Mackie, talk given at the 24-7 Prayer Conference, Portland, Oregon, October 12, 2022, quoted in *YouTube*, https://www.youtube.com/watch?v=HQIH-WfmZms.

wisdom Daniel receives doesn't come through his hard work, it's given freely when he humbly and desperately seeks God for it.

Like King Nebuchadnezzar's dream, the infinite meaning of our lives is often hidden to us. But as we surrender control in rest, silence, and stillness, we make space for eternal ideas and visions to come to us. Just as Daniel's vision was a gift, so, too, are the dreams we receive in rest. They are not earned. They are revealed.

As we rest, we awaken to the mystery of the future world. As Henri Nouwen once wrote, "The word is the instrument of the present world and silence is the mystery of the future world. If a word is to bear fruit, it must be spoken from the future world into the present world."[7]

There is an eternal rhythm beneath the surface of all things, and dormancy allows us to tap into it. The words we receive from God in solitude and silence hold an eternal weight that, when brought forth in the growing season, bears a more enduring fruit than any word we could utter on our own.

The Gift of Our True Selves

Here, in Northern Michigan, the vines spend much of the winter beneath blankets of snow and ice. While not all vineyards around the world experience such conditions, the varieties planted here thrive in them. Why? Because the snow acts as insulation. It stabilizes soil temperature, preserves moisture, and shields the roots from harsh winds, sudden freezes, and dehydration. Beneath the surface, the soil becomes a kind of enclosure—a hidden, protected space where unseen work unfolds in the roots.

---

7. Henri J.M. Nouwen, *The Way of the Heart: Connecting with God Through Prayer, Wisdom, and Silence* (New York: Ballantine Books, 1981), 52.

So it is with us. Something transformative happens in the sanctuary of solitude, creating the conditions for something new and beautiful to emerge. Carol Lee Flinders talks about this effect on the female mystics in her book, *Enduring Grace: Living Portraits of Seven Women Mystics*, describing how enclosure shaped these women, and shapes us:

> The way to awaken those sleeping parts of ourselves to life have to do with that deep inward turning. That taking up of spiritual disciplines that opens up an interior life [that] allows the sisters to start hearing her own true voice. That will be the way we can unlock the paralysis that keeps us from becoming what we want to become.[8]

Enclosure was not confinement for these women, but a place of liberation.

In silence, a different kind of knowing emerged.

In solitude, a different kind of becoming.

In stillness, a different kind of freedom.

The convent walls were not prisons; they were cocoons where these women unfolded into their truest selves. Dormancy creates space to hear that deeper voice within—the one often drowned

---

8. Carol Lee Flinders, *Enduring Grace: Living Portraits of Seven Women Mystics* (San Francisco: HarperSanFrancisco, 1993).

out by striving and the false self's need to prove. Howard Thurman captures this beautifully:

> There is something in every one of you that waits and listens for the sound of the genuine in yourself. It is the only true guide you will ever have. And if you cannot hear it, you will all of your life spend your days on the ends of strings that somebody else pulls.[9]

During winter, the vine stands bare—stripped of leaves and fruit against the backdrop of a silent vineyard. Exposed, yes, but profoundly beautiful. Here, we see the vine as it truly is.

Likewise, when our leaves and fruit fall away, when we are no longer producing or performing, we, too, begin to uncover our truest selves, and from there, our best, most authentic work emerges. It is the kind of work that, as Thurman says, is built on a "blueprint that is eternal."[10]

The Gift of New Creation

What if, unlike *the Productivity-Driven Approach* teaches us, rest was not a waste of time?

What if it's the very soil from which new creation grows?

Just consider how life emerges in the natural world:

---

9. Howard Thurman, "The Sound of the Genuine," Baccalaureate Address at Spelman College, May 4, 1980, https://thurman.pitts.emory.edu/items/show/838.

10. Howard Thurman, *Meditations of the Heart* (Boston: Beacon Press, 1953), 36.

In the hiddenness of the soil.

In the silence of the womb.

In the stillness before the world began.

Julia Cameron echoes this in *The Artist's Way*:

> Creativity—like human life itself—begins in darkness ...
> Bright ideas are preceded by a gestation period that is
> interior, murky, and completely necessary ... Ideas, like
> stalactites and stalagmites, form in the dark inner cave
> of consciousness ... All too often, we try to push, pull,
> outline, and control our ideas instead of letting them grow
> organically. The creative process is a process of surrender,
> not control.[11]

Much of my most meaningful work, the kind that carries an eternal rhythm and essence to it, was born out of extended periods of silence and solitude. But often, those seasons lasted far longer than I wished. I had to wait in the chill of winter, surrendering to the timing of spring.

Like plants, we can't force growth; we must wait until the conditions are right. When we're restless thinking, *"My dreams should have moved along by now,"* God has an eternal perspective that says, *"Not yet."* We may feel hidden, even buried, but we are not forgotten. We are being prepared for what is to come.

Yet a word of discernment is important here: not all dormancy is preparation. Sometimes, winter reveals not just a season of waiting, but a call to release. There are times when God says not "wait," but "let go." Just as some vines must be pulled up due to toxic soil, so too, we must occasionally confront what is no longer

---

11. Cameron, *The Artist's Way*, 195.

healthy or sustainable in our lives. Sometimes the soil itself needs time to lie fallow and heal before something new can grow. Discernment asks: is this waiting or releasing? Transformation or redirection?

Even so, what seems barren may be preparing for something entirely new. Something we couldn't yet imagine. And often, what appears as an ending is actually a threshold.

What if we considered dormancy a place to begin again? A place of new birth?

This is the paradox of dormancy: it feels like a kind of death, yet it is the very place where new life is formed. It is there, when the noise and clatter of the false self has been put to death, that we hear the sound of our truest selves. The one that speaks through a voice that is uniquely our own, but with the resonance of the eternal.

Digging Deeper:

1. In what ways might God be inviting you to receive the gift of rest in your life? What dreams or desires might he be awakening in you as you surrender into this rest?

2. How can you incorporate play into your life as a spiritual practice?

3. What would it look like to create space for silence and solitude to listen for the sound of your true voice?

Chapter 8:

Pruning

It's Holy Week when I visit Brigadoon Lane Vineyard in Suttons Bay. The early spring sun has begun to melt the snow. I can smell the earth thawing, but the air still carries the chill of winter. Though I can't see it yet, I know the sap has started flowing back into the vine. The life and energy stored up in dormancy is being channeled upward. The vine is on the verge of explosive growth. On the verge of resurrection.

I happen to get there just as migrant workers are finishing pruning. Their hands are quick and deliberate, clipping the branches and yanking them from the throngs of the wire trellis before tossing them on the ground. Hundreds of branches are piled up in each row. I catch sight of Dave walking up and down the rows and assessing the vines after pruning.

As I crunch through the remaining snow on my way to meet him, I clutch my phone with my frigid fingers, taking photos and documenting the losses that hit too close to home. I have solidarity with these cut branches as they remain lifeless on the snow. I've had my share of pruning moments over the years, and they all suddenly come back to the surface as I watch the clipping pile grow.

- The pruning of an unfruitful relationship

- The pruning of an opportunity I had my heart set on

- The pruning from an organization I deeply loved

- The pruning of a sin pattern that I didn't want to release

And that gnawing, biting, exposing feeling when the vine is pruned is all too familiar. It's hard to let go of branches that once hung fruit.

But in the vineyard, pruning isn't just about cutting things away. According to Dave, it "sets the intention of the vine," laying the path for growth. As I reach Dave at the end of one row, we stand in front of a Pinot Gris vine, and he says, "Pruning is the most important step in the yearly activity of cultivation because it is the foundation for the rest of the growing season. In pruning, I am telling the vine where I want it to grow."

Pruning at the Threshold

Pruning is a threshold moment. It is the space between death and resurrection, between our old selves that have died in the soil, and the new self that is waiting to emerge. Like the vine, as we journey out of seasons of dormancy and loss into spring, we feel alive again and begin to see more clearly. The life-force of the Spirit begins to flow through us and awaken us out of a spiritual slumber.

So much energy is stored up, ready to break through in spring. We have hard-earned lessons that need to manifest above ground. All the hidden work in the darkness of the soil has refined us into a new creation brimming with vitality, vigor, and vision. We are ready to grow and bear fruit for the kingdom.

But according to the wisdom of the vine, growth begins with pruning. I know—it's the worst.

When I returned from sabbatical, I found myself standing at this very threshold. My vision, once buried in the unseen work in dormancy, had begun to rise above the soil. I could finally see with greater clarity who I was and what I was called to do. Energy surged within me. I wanted to say yes to every opportunity, to partner with God in ways that would have the greatest impact. The sap of my creativity was pressing for release.

Yet just as I felt the stirring of something new, I was met with a series of painful rejections. One of the hardest came when I sought to deepen my collaboration with a ministry I had been part of for years. I longed to co-create, to offer the gifts of my art and writing in service to the community. But they chose a different path. At the time, it felt personal, and the wound cut deep.

But looking back, I can see how that closed door was, in fact, an act of pruning. It forced me to redirect my energy toward something I could not yet see. What felt like loss was, in truth, clearing the way for something greater. Had I continued down the path I had envisioned, I may never have had the creative space to pour myself into what became my first book, *Making Room in Advent*. The words and paintings that now hold so much meaning might never have come to life.

We cannot always see where or how growth will emerge, and often, we rush ahead with our own plans, eager to shape the future ourselves. But the wisdom of pruning is this: the vine-dresser alone sees the future potential. He knows exactly which branches to prune, guiding the vine's growth so it can bear the fruit it was created to yield.

Abundance Over Scarcity

As Dave and I stand before a Pinot Gris vine, he hands me a pair of pruning shears and begins to teach me the art of pruning. Before we start, he says,

> When I teach someone new how to prune, they usually don't take enough. They hesitate, caught in the "what ifs." What if I need this branch later? What if it doesn't grow back? If you don't understand what the vine is capable of, you'll prune conservatively. But, I'll remove about 90% of this vine, keeping only the 10% that will bear fruit this year and sustain next year's growth.

Ninety percent—that feels pretty drastic. And yet, as I watch Dave clip away branch after branch, I don't get the impression that he is worried about what could have been. He prunes with confidence, allowing what is cut away to fall to the ground without regret.

Why does Dave prune so aggressively? Because he knows what the vine is capable of. He trusts in the life force within it. A life force that is abundant.

Even after pruning, the vine will still produce more shoots than it can sustain. There is no point hanging onto the branches of past harvests when there is an unlimited source of growth from within.

As with us. We have the resurrection power of the Spirit within us. A limitless, powerful God flows through our veins, able to channel abundant growth.

And yet, when it comes to pruning, I often have a scarcity mindset. Like a novice vinedresser, I fixate on the 'what ifs':

What if I need that branch later?

What will happen if I let go?

What if I don't have enough?

I keep my eyes on what I can see—the branches that remain from last year's harvest—grasping tightly to opportunities, partnerships, and resources that once served me well. I want it all. So I hold on, unwilling to release control, afraid that if I let go, I'll be left with nothing.

But pruning requires surrender to a different kind of resource— one that flows from within. It calls us to trust in God's abundance and generosity. Because pruning is not merely about cutting away; it is about making space for what is yet to come.

It's the future opportunity you can't yet see as you grieve *this* pruned opportunity.

It's the spiritual maturity that grows when you let go of an unhealthy relationship.

It's the new community waiting to receive you when God leads you out of your current one.

It's the lasting impact of your time and gifts when you surrender responsibilities outside your calling.

It's the character of Christ that emerges when you allow him to prune a sin pattern.

It's the abundance that surfaces when you've given sacrificially for the sake of others.

What fruit might be on the other side of the pruning that only God can see?

What abundance, joy, or harvest might one day emerge from the very place where you now grieve being cut back?

Embracing the Limits of the Branches

Even with the Spirit's resurrection power and the abundant life of the Vine, the branches still have limits. Pruning acknowledges these limits: a vine cannot sustain both excessive growth and ripen quality grapes at the same time. Therefore, pruning is about striking a delicate balance between the vine's boundless vitality and the branch's finite capacity to channel that energy.

This principle guides Dave's work each season. As he begins pruning, he assesses each vine and ranks it from one to three based on its health and capacity for fruit-bearing:

- A vine ranked **3** has reached the top of the trellis wire and is strong enough to bear more fruit. It requires minimal pruning.

- A vine ranked **2** has only grown halfway up. It will be pruned more aggressively, and the fruit from half of the vine will be removed during the growing season to help it regain strength.

- A vine ranked **1** has experienced winter damage or trauma. It is pruned back the most, and all its fruit will be removed during the growing season so it can focus on healing. This process, known as "de-stressing," prioritizes the vine's health over immediate fruitfulness, allowing it to concentrate on roots, growth, and recovery.

In the same way, our lives are lovingly assessed by the Vinedresser, who cares more about our long-term vitality than our short-term productivity. There are seasons when we, too, have been through trauma and are simply not healthy enough to bear fruit in the ways we had envisioned.

I think of the painful losses I have experienced in my personal life or ministry that left me unable to yield a harvest. I think of my friends who have had to take a leave from work to rebuild health in their families or relationship with Jesus.

When Dave encounters a damaged vine, he is not angry at it. When he prunes and removes fruit, it isn't judgment—it's love. He loves a vine enough to invest in its future, trusting it will one day thrive without the pressure to bear fruit prematurely.

God knows we are limited. Unlike him, we cannot channel Christ's resurrection power into an unlimited number of opportunities or relationships and expect them all to be thriving and healthy. We cannot offer unlimited time, attention, and love without compromising quality.

A skilled vinedresser understands that abundance isn't measured by the number of branches, but by the quality of the fruit. As Dave explains,

> *"Grapevines are glorified weeds. If you don't prune them back, they'll produce a lot of grapes, but they won't be quality. In so many areas of our culture, we think more is better. But not in a grapevine. That mindset doesn't work if you're trying to make a really nice bottle of wine. Through pruning, we tell the vine where to put its energy, guiding it to focus on the fruit instead of wasting strength on unnecessary growth."*

Pruning cuts back the excess so that the vine can invest in what truly matters. In our lives, this might look like opportunities that don't open, relationships that change, or doors that close. Or it might mean intentionally releasing something to God's pruning shears.

At first, pruning feels like loss. All we see is what's cut away. Why remove branches that once bore fruit? Only later do we realize how essential the pruning really was. Pruning redirects our energy into fewer branches capable of producing fruit that lasts.

Vine Tears

When Dave prunes vines in early spring, he waits until the sap is flowing back into the vine. At first, this might seem counterintuitive. Why prune just as the vine is waking up? Won't this cause harm? Yet, something remarkable happens when he prunes at this time: sap begins to ooze from the wounds, forming dew-like beads. This "weeping" or "vine blood" is a natural healing agent, rich with disinfectants that protect the vine by sealing the cuts and preventing infection.

What a profound picture of the wounds of Christ.

In his suffering on the cross, we see the True Vine surrendering to the pruning process, with the "vine blood" flowing from his pierced side as a source of healing. As 1 Peter 2:24 reminds us, "By his wounds we are healed." As we abide in Christ in seasons of pruning, we can trust that the vine tears will flow freely, healing us and leading us into resurrection life.

Trellis as Support

Immediately after pruning, vinedressers here in Northern Michigan tie the vine to a trellis—a structure that provides the support it needs to grow. The trellis provides stability, allowing the vine to climb, spread out, and access the sunlight and airflow it needs. It also lifts the vine above weeds that might otherwise choke its growth or cause it to take root in the wrong places. When storms roll in, the trellis acts as an anchor, protecting the vine from damaging winds.

Tying the vine to the trellis requires a firm yet gentle hand. If the vine is pulled too hard, it can break. This delicate process demands care, wisdom, and patience, as the vinedresser carefully guides the vine's growth. Much like God does for us. When it comes to trellising, God is gentle, yet firm with us as he connects us to the right support we need to thrive.

The trellis mirrors the support systems in our spiritual lives, what St. Benedict called *a rule of life*. Just as a trellis gives structure to a vine, a rule of life shapes our formation. Our daily, weekly, and seasonal rhythms—our habits, commitments, and practices—become the framework that keeps us tethered to Christ. Without a trellis, a vine grows wildly, sprawling in every direction without purpose. Likewise, without intentional spiritual practices, we risk becoming entangled in distractions and driven by external pressures rather than rooted in the True Vine.

Choosing to live by a rule of life is an act of trust—a willingness to place ourselves in God's loving hands and be tethered to his pattern of growth. What feels limiting at first often becomes the very path to abundance.

Trellis as Restraint

Hildegard von Bingen, the 12th-century German Benedictine abbess, compared the binding of vine branches to a trellis with Christ being bound to the cross.[1] The vine's arms are outstretched along the wire, exposed to the elements without a single leaf to conceal its twisted form.

The pruned vine takes on the shape of a *T*, resembling the traditional Tau cross, which St. Francis of Assisi embraced as a symbol of humility and poverty.[2] For him, it signified a life of surrender and obedience—of being shaped, not by self-will, but by love. For St. Francis, the Tau, like the vine tied to the trellis, is an image of chosen restraint, something many of us resist.

In a *Productivity-Driven* culture that glorifies expansion and independence, we recoil at the idea of limits on growth. But intentional restraint is not punishment; it is formation.

When we feel the relentless pull toward ambition, self-reliance, or endless productivity, we are invited to surrender to the way of the cross. To practice a holy resistance and say *"no."*

---

1. Hildegard von Bingen, *Scivias*, in *Hildegard of Bingen: A Spiritual Reader*, ed. by Barbara Newman (New York: Paulist Press, 1987), 159.

2. G.K. Chesterton, *Saint Francis of Assisi* (New York: Image Books, 1957), 107.

No, we will not chase rapid growth for the sake of numbers, profit, or prestige.

No, we will not strive to prove our worth or defend our position.

No, we will not conform to the illusion of the false self.

Instead, we choose to be bound to the trellis in trust, whispering:

Even though I have my own plans for where I want to grow, I surrender to the way of love—to the way of the cross.

Peter and the Cost of Following Jesus

We see this in the story of Peter's restoration after Christ's resurrection. Though Peter was on the verge of bud break after the resurrection, Jesus knew he needed pruning.

On the beach after breakfast, Jesus asked Peter three times, "Do you love me?" mirroring Peter's three denials. After each affirmation, Jesus instructed, "Feed my sheep." Then, Jesus issued a sobering prophecy:

"Very truly I tell you, when you were younger you dressed yourself and went where you wanted; but when you are old you will stretch out your hands, and someone else will dress you and lead you where you do not want to go."[3]

---

3. John 21:18-19.

First, Jesus pruned away the shame of Peter's past failures, cutting away the very thing that could have kept him from ripening fruit. Then, he invited Peter to be tied to the trellis of sacrificial love, a path that would ultimately cost him his life. Peter resisted. Seeing John following them, he asked, "Lord, what about him?"

Jesus replied, "If I want him to remain alive until I return, what is that to you? You must follow me."[4]

Like a wild vine, Peter might have grown his own way, producing fruit of lesser quality. But, Jesus was inviting Peter to descend with him into death. Could Peter trust that this way would lead to enduring fruit?

As Peter allowed himself to be tied down to the way of the cross, he began to flourish into who he was meant to be. The man who denied Christ became the one who proclaimed him—even unto his own crucifixion upside down.

Tied to the Trellis

In my last year at seminary, I wrestled with my own calling. I lamented to my spiritual director the frustration I had been experiencing as one of the only women in the Master of Divinity program. A close friend and I were similarly gifted. We were both achievers and hard workers, studying hard and competitive with one another on all our exams and assignments. We were always neck in neck. We even shared the expository preaching award upon graduation.

But as we neared the end, I knew our journeys after seminary would look very different.

---

4. John 21:22.

His calling would never be questioned. Mine would be.

He would be offered a job as a pastor. I'd be lucky to get an interview.

He would never have to justify his presence in the pulpit; I would be asked to defend mine.

Sitting in a small room at the Dominican Center in Grand Rapids, I poured out my frustration to my spiritual director, Sharon, as I wrestled with this reality. She listened attentively and patiently waited for me to be done with my rant. Then, she gently brought me to the story in John 21, reminding me of the moment when Peter turned and looked at John and asked Jesus, "What about him?"

Like Peter, I resisted the cost. I knew obedience would mean rejection, being sidelined, and facing gender bias. As I faced the path before me, like Peter, I resisted. I looked at my friend, whistling all the way to his seemingly obstacle-less calling, and I asked "Lord, what about him?"

Jesus gently and firmly responded,
"What is that to you? You must follow me."

In many ways, living as a woman in the ministry world has felt like being pruned back and tied to the trellis in restraint. Opportunities have been limited. Rejections have been painful. Yet, in hindsight, I see how these experiences have tethered me to Jesus.

Had every opportunity been available, it would have been easy to place my confidence in my gifts or circumstances. But the pruning of rejection and the chosen restraint of obedience have led me to cling more tightly to Jesus.

Being tied to the trellis has taught me meekness—a humble, yet courageous posture to stand in the truth of who I am and Whose I am. When rejection comes, I've had to learn how to surrender to the Vinedresser's hand, allowing him to prune my growth into the shape of the kingdom; into the shape of the cross.

But let me make something clear: not all of the pruning and limitation I experienced were inherently good. Many were painful, unjust, and the result of broken systems and bad theology that have excluded women from their full calling.

Yet God, in his grace, has worked through what was painful to form something good in me.

As with the injustice of the Roman crucifixion, where the powers acted with evil intent to crucify Christ, God still brought forth the fruit of resurrection and liberation. In the same way, the unjust systems that seek to choke the callings of women are still wrong.

Toxic theologies and systems must be transformed, not justified. They, too, need careful pruning and cultivation to become cultures of wholeness, where all can thrive in their gifts. God does not require injustice to form us, but in his faithfulness, he can bring life even from the oppression that has pruned us back.

Taking the Long View

When vinedressers prune, they accept short-term loss for the sake of long-term flourishing. They are not just thinking about this season, they are thinking about the health of the vine two–three years ahead.

The same is true for the kingdom. Quality fruit doesn't ripen overnight. Growth is slow and cannot be measured by buckets spilling over with grapes. Its value is revealed in "fruit that will last."[5] Our

---

5. John 15:16.

obedience may not produce visible outcomes that we will see in our lifetime, but it contributes to an eternal harvest, nonetheless.

Unlike inanimate branches, we have a choice. At the threshold of new growth, God invites us to decide: Will we chase fruit on our own terms—throwing out branches in every direction and stretching ourselves thin across countless opportunities, relationships, and commitments in a *Productivity-Driven Approach*?

Or will we surrender to the way of flourishing—entrusting ourselves to a Vinedresser who takes the long-view, and shapes an eternal kingdom beyond what we can see?

Pruning reminds us that lasting fruitfulness starts with surrender. As we yield to the Vinedresser's pruning shears, we are prepared for the abundance of resurrection life.

Digging Deeper:

1. What are some areas in your life where you've experienced pruning, either by your own choices or external circumstances?

2. Are there any ways that, looking back, you can see how that pruning ended up producing quality fruit later?

3. What might it look like for you to surrender to the Vinedresser's care, especially in areas where pruning and being tied to the trellis feels costly?

Part III:
The Resurrection of Christ

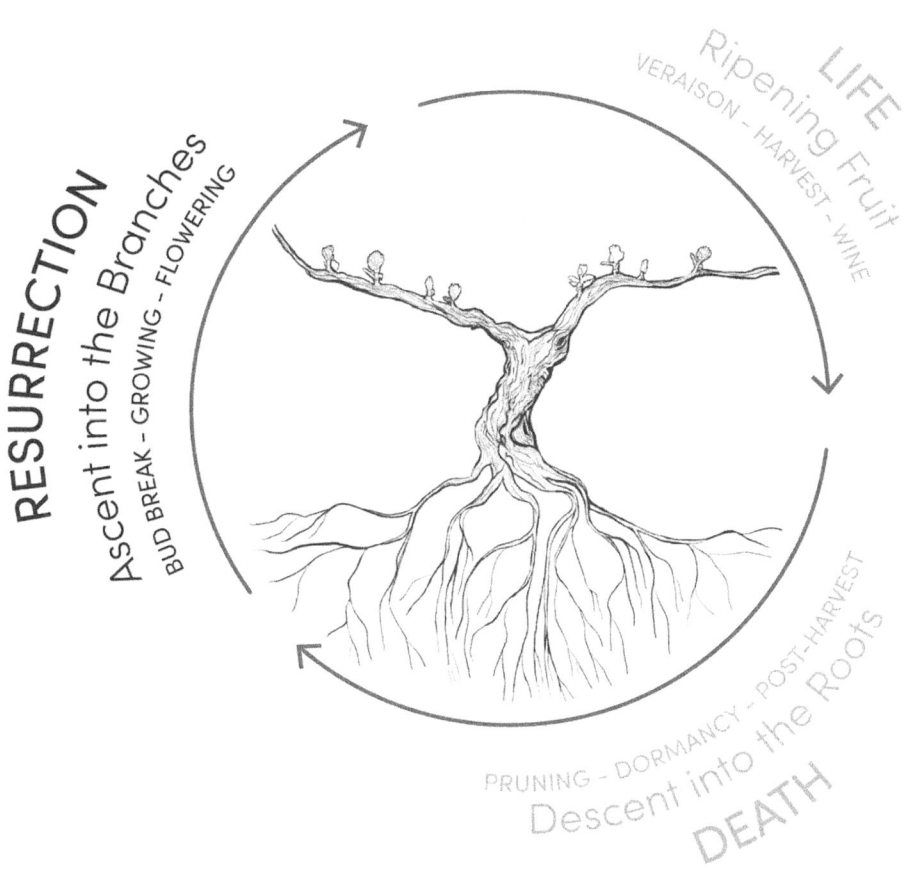

RESURRECTION

Ascent into the Branches

BUD BREAK – GROWING – FLOWERING

LIFE

Ripening Fruit

VERAISON – HARVEST – WINE

PRUNING – DORMANCY – POST-HARVEST

Descent into the Roots

DEATH

Chapter 9:

Ascent into the Branches

The early spring sun pours gold over Ten Hands Vineyard in May, casting long shadows on the grass between the vines. While the blades of grass dance in vibrant green, the vines are only just beginning to stir, waking slowly from a long winter's rest. Tiny buds unfurl along their shoulders, tentative and pale.

Dave points out the delicate leaf buds breaking through the woody canes, which were laid down on the trellis after pruning. These little buds are like quiet miracles emerging from what was unseen until now. Some leaves are cupped toward the sky, their open hands reaching to greet the sun. Others are just starting to push through, unfolding like green roses with red-tipped petals. The early buds are a pale, sage green because they are not yet actively photosynthesizing.

Dave lifts a small bud between his thumb and forefinger, holding it up for me to see. "Remember," he explains, "after the harvest, the leaves absorbed the last rays of sunshine and pushed their energy inward and downward. Now, the push for bud break comes from the energy stored in the roots."

I take a deep breath as I remember. The power for bud break doesn't come from an external source, but an internal one.

The vine bursts forth—not from the sun, not from fertilizer, but from the energy hidden in what looks like death.

The first leaves are resurrected from the reserves in the roots. And so it is with us.

Where Breakthrough Comes From

Breakthrough power—resurrection power—doesn't come from the outside.
It rises from *within*.

This is one of creation's great paradoxes.

The Productivity-Driven Approach teaches us to draw energy from external sources: financial security, positional power, influence. But, what if breakthrough doesn't come from gaining more?

What if it comes from what's already within you?

What if the power you seek isn't found in the perfect job, home, or opportunity, but has been quietly forming in the roots of your own soul?

And what if that power comes even when, or perhaps especially when, everything looks dead?

It's the very power Paul prayed we would know:

> his incomparably great power for us who believe. That power is the same as the mighty strength he exerted when he raised Christ from the dead and seated him at his right hand in the heavenly realms—far above all rule and authority, power and dominion ...[1]

That resurrection power lives in you.
And in me.

The life-giving, creative force of the God of the universe is at work through each of us.
And *that* is what causes the breakthrough.

As we tap into this resurrection power, we begin to understand what Ralph Waldo Emerson once said: "What lies behind us and what lies before us are tiny matters compared to what lies within us."[2]

The trajectory of the vine and us is this:
From dark to light
From cold to warm
From inner to outer
From soil to surface
From death to resurrection

The energy shifts from the roots to the branches.

---

1. Ephesians 1:19–21.

2. Ralph Waldo Emerson, *Essays: First Series* (Boston: James Munroe and Company, 1841), 55.

Abiding in Christ's Resurrection

So, what does it look like to abide in Christ through these seasons?

In the moments of bud break, what was once hidden within begins to burst forth into the visible world. Just as the vine inhales, drawing energy into its roots, and then exhales energy into the branches, so God's love flows in and through us.

The love we encountered as we abided in Christ in his death now rises like sap in spring. As it breaks forth, it flows outward in love for one another among the family of branches.

It's a movement from belovedness to belonging.
From solitude to community.

Jesus expresses this movement of love when he said, "Love each other as I have loved you"[3]

If the hidden seasons in the roots help us discover our identity in God's love, then the movement into the branches is how that identity gets expressed in community. As our inner life awakens, it doesn't stay hidden. It begins to take shape in the world around us—in our actions, relationships, and creative expression—as we love one another.

Bud Break as Incarnation

This is the shift from inspiration to incarnation—when the Word becomes flesh through us.

The word "inspiration" comes from the Latin word *inspiratus*, which essentially means "breathe into." It is the divine breath of God filling our lungs and finding form in the world through the unique

---

3. John 15:12.

expression of who we are. Inspiration becomes incarnation when God's presence manifests through our presence in the world.

> **When we pursue the dreams once buried in the quiet corners of our hearts,**
> **God's dreams take on flesh.**
>
> **When we find our own voice and use it, others begin to hear God's voice through us.**
>
> **And when we risk being fully seen, miraculous breakthroughs follow.**

Julia Cameron calls this concept *synchronicity* in her book, *The Artist's Way*. She explains that when we dare to own our gifts and step into God's call on our lives—even when no opportunity lies before us—the world opens to us. Like the vine opening its leaves to the sun, we open ourselves and receive the energy of the Spirit. As we do, a surge of life bursts forth that cannot be stopped, bringing exponential growth, abundance, and joy. As Cameron puts it, "leap, and the net will appear."[4]

One such moment of synchronicity unfolded when I chose to create—not because someone had asked, and not because a door had opened—but simply because I *had* to. That's when I met Danielle.

Encountering God's Boundless Love in Community

Danielle Strickland inspired me long before I met her. From a distance, I was captivated by her prophetic leadership—how she

---

4. Cameron, *The Artist's Way*, 57.

sows seeds of possibility into the most hostile, unjust environments. Her relentless pursuit of justice, paired with a buoyant, Spirit-led vision for the future, has birthed countless initiatives that push back darkness with light.

Take *Brave*,[5] for example, an organization that tackles human trafficking at its roots by empowering the most vulnerable populations: young girls in the foster care system. Or *IMBY* (*In My Back Yard*),[6] which addresses both the affordable housing crisis and the loneliness epidemic by building tiny homes in people's yards—sparking creativity, play, and connection.

Danielle and I first met through a virtual monthly prayer day she hosted with Infinitum,[7] a discipleship practice she co-founded. Infinitum acts like a root system, nourishing the many initiatives Danielle has started by helping its leaders abide in Jesus and embody his life through surrender, generosity, and others-centered mission.

Not long after joining the prayer day as a participant, I offered some artwork and prayer resources I had previously created for the team to use during their gatherings. After a few collaborations with Infinitum, Danielle invited me to join her team as artist-in-residence.

It was a pivotal moment for me. For the first time, someone I deeply admired invited me to contribute in the very way I felt

---

5. Brave Global – Empowers vulnerable girls in foster care to prevent human trafficking. https://braveglobal.org

6. IMBY Homes (In My Back Yard) – Creates affordable housing and fosters community by building tiny homes in residential yards. https://www.imby-homes.org

7. Infinitum Life – A discipleship movement that helps people centered their lives on Jesus and live like him through the practices of surrender, generosity, and mission. https://infinitumlife.com

uniquely called—but was rarely asked—to bring my creativity to the table.

It was the inner work I had done during sabbatical that helped me to own this gift and show up unapologetically to serve others with it. When I took a leap, the net appeared. And that net was a community of leaders from Danielle's many initiatives that were slowly weaving into something new: *Boundless*,[8] a family that embraced me not just for what I could do, but for who I was.

A Sacred Belonging Among Misfits

What made that moment even more significant wasn't just the opportunity to work with Danielle, it was the invitation into a community shaped by a new way of being. The leaders of *Boundless* were intentionally cultivating an alternative to *the Productivity-Driven Approach* that had formed so many of us. The deeper I have sunk into this community, the more God has liberated me from the patterns and pressures of that old way.

This shift really began to take root when Danielle gathered us for our first *Boundless* retreat in 2022 in Orlando, Florida. On the first day, we sat in a circle around a pool as each leader shared their story: what had brought them to *Boundless*, what inspired them to launch their initiatives, and what they had hoped for the future.

As I listened, I scanned the faces of our little *Boundless* community of leaders from around the world and couldn't help but

8. Boundless Enterprise, "About Boundless," accessed October 30, 2024, https://www.boundlessenterprise.org/who-we-are.

think how much we looked like a little *Island of Misfit Toys*.[9] A consistent theme emerged in our stories: most of us hadn't fit into the traditional molds of church or organizational life. We were artists, people of color, neurodivergent leaders, sensitive men, and women who had been marginalized from these spaces.

There we were, square pegs who had bounced out of round holes, scattered across the ceramic floor of that makeshift sanctuary, only to discover a sacred sense of belonging among fellow misfits.

Before the retreat, Danielle and our team talked about how to structure our time. Should we work on projects together? Map out goals? Talk about our vision and strategy? But then, Danielle said something that shifted everything:

"I think this community already knows how to get things done. What they really need is to know that they are loved."

And that's exactly what happened. We experienced being seen, soothed, safe, and secure by one another. We felt cherished and loved unconditionally, apart from anything we produced. In fact, there wasn't really much talk about what was accomplished throughout the year on our teams—and we accomplished a lot.

What we celebrated was *us*—individually and collectively.

We spent a little time making plans and dreaming together about upcoming opportunities. But you know what we spent the *most* time doing?

We shared meals together. We laughed—a lot. We danced. We sang karaoke and played Family Feud™ games. We practiced

---

9. The *Island of Misfit Toys* is a location in *Rudolph the Red-Nosed Reindeer*, directed by Larry Roemer (Rankin/Bass Productions, 1964), television special.

the posture of surrender by floating in the pool. We made ridiculous infomercials for one another's initiatives that were both hilarious and moving. We prayed and dreamed together. We listened to God for one another.

We spent time intentionally getting to know one another—not for networking purposes, not to strategize, but simply to welcome, to love, and to understand. To behold one another. To delight in one another. And to recognize how deeply we really need one another.

As I experienced being seen, soothed, safe, and secure by this beloved community, I began to let my guard down and relax into true self. I no longer felt the need to prove, perform, or strive for love and belonging, because I already had it. It was freely given, always available, and abundant. It was *Boundless.*

From Productivity to Flourishing: A Different Way of Community

In that sacred space of belonging, I found that all parts of myself could come to the table: the prophetic side, the contemplative side, the goofy and giggly sides, the creative side, and even the achiever. I felt free to belt out *"Part of Your World"* from *The Little Mermaid* one moment and rap to *"My Shot"* from *Hamilton* the next. And every part was embraced.

In Chapter 2, we explored how being seen, soothed, safe, and secure in God forms a secure attachment—a deep bond of communion with him. When we grow up from those roots into a community that sees and holds us in the same way, we form relational attachments that ripen quality fruit.

The first *Boundless* retreat marked the beginning of that kind of community for our team. The deep relational connections formed there have sustained us across time zones and continents. And it's from these relationships that we've found the support, nourishment, and inspiration to continue the gritty work of justice and healing in our various contexts.

It's important to note the intentional flow of this: relationship before fruit. We are a team of hard workers, deeply shaped by *the Productivity-Driven Approach*. Many of us have found it hard to rest or separate our identities from our output. But these retreats have helped us practice *the Flourishing Approach*, which prioritizes rest, play, connection, and belonging.

As we invest in these relationships, something mysterious happens: we begin to rise into our truest selves. The overflow is a harvest of quality fruit that is expressed not only in what we create together, but in the kind of community we become. The fruit doesn't always arrive on the fast-paced timeline that *the Productivity-Driven Approach* demands. But when it comes, it's richer and more lasting, because it's been cultivated through the long, slow, relational rhythm of *the Flourishing Approach*.

Two Targets: What Are We Really Aiming For?

Psychiatrist and neuroscientist Jim Wilder, along with spiritual leader Marcus Warner, explore this tension in their book *Rare Leadership: 4 Uncommon Habits for Increasing Trust, Joy, and Engagement in the People You Lead*. They identify two primary targets that leaders typically aim for:

1. Getting Results
This is the dominant mode in Western leadership. This form of leadership prioritizes management and problem solving. When we put results as the primary target, Wilder and Warner write, "we focus on things like making a profit, winning games, expanding our market, and growing our ministry. For many of us,

such a focus seems so self-evident that we never even consider there might be an alternative."[10] This is *the Productivity-Driven Approach* on full display.

However, Wilder and Warner warn that when results are the primary goal, "we create a fear-based motivation for our performance. The result is a toxic environment characterized by low motivation, low bonding, and low excellence with little reason to sacrifice for the greater good."[11] This is where people burn out—when the soil of our souls gets malnourished from overproduction and low relational connection.

2. Building a Group Identity

The alternative target is often overlooked: cultivating a group identity. This means building a relationally nourishing culture that answers the questions: *Who are we?* and *What is it like for us to act?*

This echoes what we explored in Chapter 3. Our character (who we are becoming) is formed more by our relational attachments than by our beliefs. We may have a strong mission statement, but if we don't have strong relational attachments, we won't be motivated to live into it. When identity comes first, the other target—getting results—follows naturally.

Wilder and Warner point to Morgan Wootten, a legendary high-school basketball coach. Wooten consistently got winning results; however, this was not his primary target. His target was a *culture of transformation*. Often, Wootten would have one of his players living with his family, forming strong relational bonds with his

---

10. Marcus Warner and Jim Wilder, *Rare Leadership: 4 Uncommon Habits for Increasing Trust, Joy, and Engagement in the People You Lead* (Chicago: Moody Publishers, 2016), 91.

11. Warner and Wilder, *Rare Leadership*, 92.

team, and as Wilder and Warner add: "unlike coaches who used their players to build their programs, he used his program to change the lives of his players."[12]

Models of a *Flourishing Approach* to Leadership

This way of leadership is counter-cultural and rare, but not absent. Here are a few leaders who prioritized group identity and saw fruit as a result:

- **Jesus:** His ministry wasn't focused on growing a large following, but on the formation of his disciples. He wasn't interested in creating workhorses for the kingdom, he was interested in cultivating friends. Jesus sought to build a transformative community grounded in love, humility, and service. Over time, this community, empowered by the Holy Spirit, spread like wildfire and changed the world.

- **Mother Teresa:** Her order didn't set out to "solve" poverty. They simply sought to love and serve the poor with dignity and compassion. But the ministry Mother Teresa created has inspired thousands, leading to international change for individuals and communities.[13]

- **Pixar Studios:** Known for creative excellence, Pixar's secret sauce isn't perfectionism, it's psychological safety. It has become known for creating trust and collaboration among their team members. By focusing on the

---

12. Warner and Wilder, *Rare Leadership*, 91.

13. Malcolm Muggeridge, *Something Beautiful for God* (New York: Harper & Row, 1971), 42.

team's health, identity, and growth, Pixar has consistently achieved success in the film industry.[14]

- ✎ **Fred Rogers:** Host of *Mister Rogers' Neighborhood*, Mr. Rogers didn't seek high ratings or commercial success, but focused on building a culture of kindness, understanding, and emotional connection for children. As a result of prioritizing the well-being and development of his young audience, his program has had a profound impact.[15]

As Wilder and Warner write, when cultivating a group identity is the target, this kind of community is motivated by joy, and their members understand that "excellence is just part of being who they are and what they do."[16] When we belong to a community that cultivates strong relational attachments within a shared identity, we offer our best selves, and in turn, our best work.

Breaking Free from the Productivity Trap

In Western culture, we're conditioned to believe that productivity equals worth. We're taught that success is tied to individual achievement, that output defines identity, and that the ends of reaching goals justifies the means of oppression and exploitation.

Many of us have had the visceral experience of working in a toxic culture like this. We've felt the drain of transactional relationships,

---

14. Ed Catmull and Amy Wallace, *Creativity, Inc.: Overcoming the Unseen Forces That Stand in the Way of True Inspiration* (New York: Random House, 2014), 87.

15. Maxwell King, *The Good Neighbor: The Life and Work of Fred Rogers* (New York: Abrams Press, 2018), 112.

16. Warner and Wilder, *Rare Leadership*, 92.

the disillusionment of being used, and the burnout that comes when excellence is demanded without nourishment or care.

This distorted mindset often mirrors what we learned in high school: Maslow's Hierarchy of Needs. It tells us that once we've worked our way up the ladder—from basic needs to self-esteem—we'll eventually reach the top: *self-actualization*. It mirrors the American Dream: work hard enough, and you'll become your best self, living a happier, more fulfilled life.

From Self-Actualization to Communal Flourishing

Later in life, though, Maslow had a reckoning with this model. After spending time with the Blackfoot people, an Indigenous North American tribe traditionally located in Alberta, Canada and Montana, he recognized a different paradigm.

During six weeks with the Blackfoot community, Maslow observed that "80–90% of the tribal members had a level of self-esteem found in only 5–10% of his own population."[17] Among the Blackfoot, self-actualization was not something to be earned, it was assumed at birth. Everyone was inherently worthy of love and belonging, contributing something valuable to society simply by being themselves.

In their worldview, self-actualization was at the bottom of their pyramid. The pinnacle wasn't individual success, but *communal actualization*: the thriving of the whole community.

This vision resonates deeply with the Christian understanding of being created in the image of God. Like the Blackfoot, we believe

---

17. Teju Ravilochan, "The Blackfoot Wisdom that Inspired Maslow's Hierarchy," *Resilience.org*, June 18, 2021, https://www.resilience.org/stories/2021-06-18/the-blackfoot-wisdom-that-inspired-maslows-hierarchy/.

that worth is not something to earn, but something we inherently carry as God's beloved image-bearers. Our task is not to strive for worth, but to remember it. As we recover our identity in God's love in our roots, we naturally arise into the community of branches with a shared sense of belonging and purpose.

With self-actualization at the foundation of the pyramid, for the Blackfoot people, the highest goal was to contribute to the well-being of the whole community. Wealth, in their view, was not measured by accumulation, but by generosity. As they saw it, "the wealthiest man is one who has almost nothing because he has given it all away."[18]

The Posture of Generosity: Christ's Resurrected Community

When the power of Christ's resurrection begins to take root in our lives, our focus shifts from self-actualization to *communal* actualization. We begin to reflect the kind of community described in Acts, where "all who believed were together and had all things in common. They sold their possessions and distributed the proceeds to all, as any had need."[19]

Just as the Blackfoot measured wealth by generosity, the early church was marked by a spirit of shared abundance and belonging. When we recognize that we belong to each other, generosity becomes the natural fruit of our shared life.

---

18. D. Coon, quoted in Teju Ravilochan, "The Blackfoot Wisdom that Inspired Maslow's Hierarchy," *Resilience.org*, June 18, 2021, https://www.resilience. org/stories/2021-06-18/the-blackfoot-wisdom-that-inspired-maslows-hierarchy/.

19. Acts 2:44-45.

When we grasp our inherent place in God's family, the question is no longer, *"What must I do to earn my belonging?"* but rather, *"I already belong, so what can I give?"*

The Flourishing Approach embraces an abundance mindset: freely we have received, so freely we give. Instead of living from scarcity or striving, we begin to live from love and belonging.

This doesn't mean abandoning tasks or goals, but grounding them in relationships of trust, generosity, and shared purpose. When people feel seen and valued, collaboration flows. Team meetings shift from transactional to transformational—not because the work doesn't matter, but because healthy relationships create the conditions where our best work can emerge.

Instead of a checklist mentality that treats people as a means to an end, we cultivate conversations that draw out the wisdom, creativity, and diverse perspectives of our team members. Leadership becomes less about control and more about empowerment. People step in to help without being asked because the good of the whole matters more than individual gain.

When the wellbeing of the community is the aim, people genuinely *want* to work together. They find joy in being part of something bigger than themselves. In this environment, progress may be slower, but its impact endures.

As followers of Jesus, we're called to seek communal flourishing over self-actualization. In the kingdom of God, when we tend to the health, quality, and vitality of our relationships—like Dave tends to his vines—good fruit follows.

Digging Deeper:

1. What are some desires God has awakened you to that he wants you to incarnate into the world?

2. What have you freely received from God? How might he be inviting you to freely extend that to others?

3. How have you seen *the Flourishing Approach* or *the Productivity-Driven Approach* play out in the communities in which you are a part? Who models a *Flourishing Approach* to leadership that you can learn from?

Chapter 10:

Bud Break

I arrive at Ten Hands Vineyard with my family just after Mother's Day. I want to get a glimpse of the vines again during bud break. As my two boys run around the vineyards with my husband, I study the Riesling vines carefully. Several small green nubs poke their little heads out from the branches tied to the trellis. Some of the buds have just barely unfolded and are nearly translucent. The morning sun shines through them, and reveals the tiny veins pulsing sap through leaves no bigger than my thumb. They stretch up toward the sky, opening like a clam shell and revealing a spiral of yet-to-bloom leaves.

I focus my camera on the tiny zig-zagged ridges of each leaf and wonder how something so small and fragile can push through the hard surface of the cane. My boys, laughing and shouting, run toward me, elbowing for my attention. They each take turns standing between me and the vines, making silly faces and posing with their arms outstretched like vines themselves so I can photograph them. And I remember how small things can sometimes pack a mighty punch.

Breaking Through Resistance

At bud break, the life force of the vine must push through a thick protective layer in order to emerge into the light. The nature of breakthrough is that it must *break through* something. Every act of new life and creation is accompanied by resistance. It's just the nature of all things. We see this pattern all over creation on the cusp of new beginnings:

Little seedlings must burst forth from the cracks in the shell.

A butterfly must thrust open its chrysalis in order to fly.

A baby chick must push through the egg shell to be born.

An artist must crack through the fear of a blank canvas for a piece to emerge.

As Steven Pressfield writes in *The War of Art: Break through the Blocks and Win Your Inner Creative Battles*:

"Rule of thumb: The more important a call or action is to our soul's evolution, the more Resistance we will feel toward pursuing it."[1]

---

1. Steven Pressfield, *The War of Art: Break Through the Blocks and Win Your Inner Creative Battles* (New York: Black Irish Entertainment, 2002), 12.

I felt this resistance acutely toward the end of my sabbatical.

As I shared in earlier chapters, God had done a lot of internal work to recover the frightened and vulnerable artist within. The more I practiced creating, the stronger that identity became. But when it came time for my sabbatical to be over, I had to push through all kinds of resistance internally and externally in order to own this identity.

Do you remember the image God gave me of my prophetic artistic gift as wings?

Every time I encountered obstacles in using my gifts, it felt like a giant rubber band was wrapped around them. Pushing against that tension was like resistance band training. Each time I pushed back against the pull of the rubber band, my wings stretched further and grew stronger. And, much like a baby bird emerging from its egg, that strength training was exactly what I would need to eventually take flight.

During my sabbatical, I collaborated with my employer to craft a role that allowed me to create spiritual formation resources through my art and writing. But, because of the COVID-19 pandemic, we were in a hiring freeze. The position still needed executive-level approval, and it wasn't clear whether it would ever become available.

As I listened to my potential supervisor explain the uncertainty of the situation to me, my body clenched up in fear. A part of me wanted to give up. I could have chosen the safer path, settling for a job that didn't include my art.

But all of a sudden, something rose up within me—a sort of confidence, courage, and resilience I had not experienced before. It was as if my artist soul drew a line in the sand and said, "No, I will no longer be put in a box." For the first time in my life, instead of withdrawing or shapeshifting to belong, I simply said:

"Well, whether or not there is a position for me, I know this is what I was created to do. So if it works for me to take this position, great. If not, I will find some other way."

I *never* would have said that before sabbatical. In the past, I would have caved and tried to change who I was to accommodate the limits of my environment. But something was breaking through in me. New life was emerging.

Resistance is a testing ground. It calls for deep-rooted confidence in the truth of who God says we are, and trust in his resurrection power at work within us. That inner strength, formed in hidden seasons and nourished by our connection to the True Vine, is essential for becoming the new creation we're meant to be.

Jesus and the Weight of Resistance

Jesus intimately knew the experience of resistance. At his baptism, he was filled with the Holy Spirit, and the Father affirmed his identity: *"You are my beloved Son; with you I am well pleased."*[2] Rooted in this divine affirmation, Jesus immediately entered the wilderness, where he had to confront intense resistance and temptation from Satan. Even with the clarity of his identity, he had to wrestle to fully embody it.

After the wilderness, Jesus publicly declared his mission by reading from Isaiah 61: "The Spirit of the Lord is on me, because he has anointed me to proclaim good news to the poor. He has sent me to proclaim freedom for the prisoners and recovery of sight for the blind, to set the oppressed free, to proclaim the year of the Lord's favor."[3]

---

2. Luke 3:22.

3. Luke 4:18–19.

Initially, his words were met with admiration. But, when he challenged the assumptions of his audience by suggesting that God's blessing extended beyond Israel to the Gentiles, the crowd turned on him. Their praise quickly turned to fury, and they tried to throw him off a cliff.[4]

Even in the face of rejection in his hometown by his own people, Jesus remained grounded in his identity as God's beloved Son. He did not bend to the pressure of public opinion or seek validation from the crowd. Instead, he stayed faithful to the mission he had been given.

Likewise, as we emerge from our own seasons of dormancy into the call God has placed on our lives, we will often face resistance. Old patterns, familiar voices, or external pressures will try to pull us back into our false selves. But, in moments of criticism, rejection, failure, or loss, we must choose to stand firm in our identity as God's beloved, seeking his approval alone, no matter what may come.

The moment of emergence into our true selves is both powerful and vulnerable.

Bud Break as Courageous Vulnerability

The vine gives us a picture of this paradox in the process of bud break. While it takes tremendous strength for a leaf bud to push through the resistance of the branch and burst into the light, what emerges is incredibly delicate. Even a gentle push of the vinedresser's thumb can cause the bud to fall off the vine. During this time, the vine is also most at risk of frost damage, which can impact the future harvest.

---

4. Luke 4:29.

Bud break is a symbol of *courageous vulnerability.*

And we get this, right? It is vulnerable to emerge into who we were made to be amidst a climate storming with criticism, differing viewpoints, and systems that may or may not be expecting us to show up in our full, beautiful selves. We can feel like a five-year-old on the first day of kindergarten—timid, insecure, and exposed.

Bud break is the courage to begin again.

It's the first day at a new job after the fallout from the last one.
It's the moment you realize you're pregnant after multiple miscarriages.
It's the first date after a string of several heartbreaks.
It's the manuscript you dare to write after three rejections.
It's the ministry you plant after the fallout from the last.

And through it all, the questions quietly echo:

Will I bear the fruit I believe I'm called to bear?

Will there be room for this dream? For me?

Will anyone believe in this small, sacred thing I carry in my heart, the one so precious I can barely name?

As Brené Brown says, "Courage starts with showing up and letting ourselves be seen."[5]

It takes courage to rise after a long winter of drought, disappointment, or failure.

To keep going when everything in you says, *"You never should have started in the first place."*

To keep showing up—even when the world says it's not worth it. Even when past records confirm the doubt.

But, despite all this resistance, bud break is one of the most rare and beautiful moments in life. While, outwardly, a single green shoot breaking through may not look like much, every time, it feels like a miracle.

Because it is.

The Inner Strength for Breakthrough

When we cling to Christ, staying attached to the Vine in the dark soil where no light can reach, something sacred begins to take shape deep within. Something hidden. Something holy. Something that will one day break forth with resurrection power.

> It's the strength formed in the roots when you keep praying, even when God is silent.

> It's what grows in the dark when you nurture a dream, even when it looks dead.

---

5. Brené Brown, *Daring Greatly: How the Courage to Be Vulnerable Transforms the Way We Live, Love, Parent, and Lead* (New York: Gotham Books, 2012), 47.

It's what gathers at the edge of outstretched tendrils when you reach for water in a drought.

It's the perseverance cultivated in the tomb of suffering, when you choose to remain with Jesus rather than numb or flee.

Bud break reminds us: what looks fragile on the surface has deep roots.

Only God knows what it took to get to bud break—the years of going nowhere but down—into silence, into solitude, into dormancy, into dying to the false self, so something truer could emerge.

The energy accumulated in the roots through surrender and waiting is released into the branches with resurrection power.

And to channel *that* kind of power requires an undivided heart.

A surrendered heart.

A heart that trusts in the strength of God alone.

That's why we need seasons of dormancy: to surrender our own power so we can receive a greater one.

While we are exposed and vulnerable at bud break, we can break through confidently because those many months of dormancy have prepared us. That quiet inner voice we've been learning to trust in the darkness now asks to be heard in the light. The branch must emerge into what it was always designed to be.

As John O'Donohue writes:

> It is in the depths of your life that you will discover the invisible necessity that has brought you here. When you begin to decipher this, your gift and giftedness come alive. Your heart quickens and the urgency of living rekindles your creativity. If you can awaken this sense of destiny, you come into rhythm with your life.[6]

Unfolding from Our True Self

Several months before my sabbatical ended, I sat across from one of my ministry partners, Brad, at an outdoor patio in downtown Traverse City. Over breakfast, I shared with him how I felt called to create resources using my art and writing to facilitate spaces of encounter and transformation with Jesus. But I also shared how hard it had been to find a place for that kind of work within the systems I had been part of. No one seemed to be asking for what I had to give.

Brad, the CEO of a marketing firm, listened and responded, "Bette, what you're describing is incredibly differentiated. In the marketing world, that's a very good thing."

Something clicked.

In that moment, my posture shifted. What I had interpreted as a sign that I didn't belong because "no one is doing what I'm doing" suddenly became a sign that I had something valuable to offer. Something uniquely needed.

---

6. John O'Donohue, *Anam Cara: A Book of Celtic Wisdom* (New York: HarperCollins, 1997), 74.

Instead of seeing my distinctiveness as a liability, I began to recognize it as an asset, a gift that could serve others who needed it.

This is the power of community among the branches of The Vine. When others see something in us and call it forth with encouragement, affirmation, or a fresh perspective, it gives us the courage to step more fully into who we are. While solitude helps us uncover our true voice, it is in community that our voice is called to arise.

We all have a deep desire to belong. But it can be hard to show up in our true selves, especially if what we offer is different. Still, what if it's our difference that makes a difference? What if the very thing that sets us apart is exactly what the world desperately needs?

When a vine commits to blossom and yields the fruit it alone was made to bear, it naturally attracts those who long for that specific taste. It doesn't strive to be something else. It simply *is* what it was created to be.

The same is true for you.

Can you trust that there are people who need the real you?
Can you believe the world aches for your true self to emerge?

As Howard Thurman famously said, "Don't ask what the world needs. Ask what makes you come alive, and go do it. Because what the world needs is people who have come alive."[7]

We need fewer people conforming to molds and more people owning their unique and creative voice in the world. Because

---

7. Howard Thurman, *The Living Wisdom of Howard Thurman: A Visionary for Our Time* (Minneapolis, MN: Fortress Press, 1999), 116.

when we begin to own who we are, those who are looking for us will finally be able to find us.

Your true self, your dream, your calling, may not be something the world seems to be asking for right now. But when you have discovered it from the sacred source within, from your attachment to the True Vine, and if it bursts forth with the strength only God provides, then you can be sure that the world needs it. Even if it doesn't know it yet.

Yet, how we unfold from that fragile bud break stage depends a lot on the communities we experience among our neighboring branches. Are we welcomed to unfold into our truest selves in the spaces we inhabit? And do we offer that same welcome to others? Or do we belong only if we perform a certain way, dress a certain way, or produce specific results?

When our belonging feels conditional, like a fragile bud opening in spring only to be met by a late winter frost, our growth can quickly shut down. We retreat into our false selves, shapeshifting into what we think is acceptable in order to be loved. But this isn't true belonging, is it? As Brené Brown writes, "True belonging doesn't require you to change who you are; it requires you to *be* who you are."[8]

And yet, many of us live in environments where this kind of belonging feels out of reach.

The Crisis of Disconnection

While *the Flourishing Approach* seeks to cultivate communities where each unique individual can thrive in connection with

---

8. Brené Brown, *Braving the Wilderness: The Quest for True Belonging and the Courage to Stand Alone* (New York: Random House, 2017), 40.

one another, one of the tragic effects of *the Productivity-Driven Approach* is disconnection. We have become independent, but we have forgotten how desperately we need one another. The loneliness epidemic is outpacing most other epidemics in scope and severity.[9]

Dr. Bruce Perry, psychiatrist and co-author with Oprah Winfrey of *What Happened to You?*, underscores this reality. "Disconnection and loneliness in our society are playing a major role in the increased anxiety, sleep problems, substance abuse, and depression we're seeing," he writes. "A recent Harvard study confirms that social connection is one of the most powerful protectors against depression, even for those with genetic predispositions or trauma histories."[10]

In exploring how connection contributes to healing, Dr. Perry spent time with the Māori community in New Zealand. Through studying their deeply interdependent community, he began to understand that, from their perspective, pain and dysfunction often arise from fragmentation and disconnection.

He explains, "A core element of their traditional healing practices is *'whanaungatanga,'* which refers to reciprocal relationships, kinship, and a sense of family connection. These practices involve reconnecting with family, community, and the natural world."[11] In contrast, he notes that Western medicine often misses the mark by focusing on compartmentalized health. "If connectedness is

---

9. Stephen Smith, "The Loneliness Epidemic: Analyzing the Current State of Social Isolation," *Journal of Social and Personal Relationships* 37, no. 5 (2022): 121–135.

10. Bruce Perry and Oprah Winfrey, *What Happened to You?* (New York: Flatiron Books, 2021), 261.

11. Perry and Winfrey, *What Happened to You?*, 250.

not addressed," he says, "the effectiveness of Western interventions is diminished."[12]

Healing, then, is not just about therapy—it's about reintegration through meaningful relationships. "Having access to a number of invested, caring people is a better predictor of healing after trauma than having access to a therapist," Perry notes. "The therapeutic web—positive, relational-based opportunities throughout your day—is crucial."[13]

We cannot be fully healed without experiencing that healing and restoration in community. We have to take the risk to show up, to be seen, to be loved, because the truth is: others need us. And we need them.

This kind of interdependence is woven into the very fabric of creation.

Cover Crops

During a lecture at the Elk Rapids Garden Club, Dave explained the practice of cover cropping: "It's the idea of using a living plant to heal another living plant. A hundred years ago, this was just a given. Healthy and diverse relationships between vines and other crops make them more resilient to diseases like black rot and mildew, and they heal faster. Cover cropping is a cornerstone of what we're trying to do to bring health, quality, and vitality to the plant."

Different plants contribute in different ways. For example, legumes enrich the soil by infusing nitrogen, a key nutrient for growth.

---

12. Perry and Winfrey, What Happened to You?, 250.

13. Perry and Winfrey, What Happened to You?, 230.

Mustard plants, with their deep taproots, help prevent erosion and make buried nutrients more accessible to future crops.

After the talk, Dave pulled me aside and said, "Isn't it amazing how deeply relational our Creator made all things? He is no less intentional with us."

The more I reflect on it, the more I see how true this is. When we are truly embraced as we are, our presence offers the nutrients someone else needs, and we receive theirs in return. As discussed in earlier chapters, healing happens in these mutual exchanges, where we are seen, soothed, safe, and secure.

My Cover Crop Family

I experienced this healing first-hand a few years ago. I had just come through an intense season of writing, most of it spent in isolation. While this time of solitude is critical to the kind of work I do, over time, I've realized that if I spend too much time alone, my soul becomes depleted and malnourished. Like an isolated vine, I'm less resilient against challenges that come my way. One week, after facing yet another rejection as an artist and a woman in ministry, I felt drained and discouraged.

Thankfully, that weekend I attended one of our *Boundless* retreats. I arrived early, trying to pray, but couldn't focus. I was too distracted from the stressful situation. But then I sensed God saying, *"Bette, I want to speak to you and restore you, but I am going to do so through community. Just rest."*

When the team arrived, something immediately shifted in me. Without words, I felt embraced as a beloved part of the community. We laughed, caught up, shared stories, danced, and simply delighted in one another's company. I was reminded that whether or not I fit into traditional structures, I belonged here—among this community of misfits.

Like a cover crop replenishing depleted soil, their presence nourished me. We prayed for one another, listened to God on each other's behalf, and shared words of encouragement. When they prayed over me, they reminded me of my prophetic calling and urged me not to shrink back in fear but to step forward in the authority God has given me. They reminded me of God's delight in me and the call to use my gifts and voice no matter the response from others.

During our last meal together, I spoke with three men from our community about my painful experience as a woman in ministry. They listened empathetically without judgment, grieved with me, and affirmed that I wasn't crazy. Their response was healing in a way I didn't expect. After so many wounds tied to male power and exclusion, these brothers offered the opposite impulse—a posture of humility, empathy, and honor. That ten-minute conversation gave me the healing and strength I needed to return to my work with resilience, compassion, and confidence.

We all need this: a safe community where we can belong, be nourished, and find healing.

God has woven a web of interdependent relationships throughout creation. Each of us is a unique masterpiece, carrying gifts meant to sustain and bless others. And we, too, have needs we cannot meet alone. This is mutuality—a foundational principle in God's vineyard.

Digging Deeper:

1. What are some areas you've experienced resistance when creating something new?

2. What would it look like to demonstrate "courageous vulnerability" to bring your true self into community?

3. Who is your "cover crop family"? Are there people in your life who have infused the nutrients you need to grow?

Notes

Chapter 11:

Growing

It's a balmy 80-degree day in June when I walk through Brigadoon Lane Vineyard after a writing retreat. Ed and Adina, the owners, have been tending this small acre of Pinot Gris and Merlot vines for the past five years. When I arrive, Adina is sitting in front of a vine, perched on an upside-down, five-gallon bucket, gently pulling off several shoots from the vine with her hands.

The vines that had once looked shy and unobtrusive during bud break, like a small child hiding behind her mother, have now opened up into full, wild extroversion. The leaves are spread flat and broad, and the branches are throwing out leaves and lateral shoots every which way without restraint, like a teenager sporting a moppy haircut.

It is as though the vine has been waiting for this—waiting for a time so it could grow unhindered and free with no regard for how or where, only that it grows. Several tendrils of the vine have wrapped around the wire trellis in a curl, grasping it as if to prepare for another flying leap toward the sky.

Dave walks over, points to the sprawling vines and explains, "From bud break until flowering, a vine can grow inches a day. It's not thinking at all about fruit—only about growing."

Turning toward the Sun

There comes a point, just after the tender vulnerability of bud break, when everything shifts. The first leaves, having pushed through, now unfurl and begin to photosynthesize, drawing energy from the sun. It's a turning point—the vine is no longer relying solely on internal reserves. Now, external forces are fueling its growth, propelling it forward with rapid and abundant momentum.

In the same way, when we emerge from a season of dormancy and turn our faces toward the sun, we open ourselves to receive the many gifts the Spirit brings. We are energized by these resources that fuel us with energy and light.

After a long stretch of waiting or struggle, we finally experience a breakthrough. We wake up with a spring in our step. We have our energy back. It seems like nothing could dampen our spirits. The depression has lifted and our vision is clarified. We stay up later because we are filled with new ideas. We try new things, build new relationships, and start new, God-inspired ventures. We have passed through winter's chill and now we are ready to grow outward. And we can't wait to get started.

We've all had moments like this, right?

When you get so engrossed in a project that you forget to eat.

When you feel a surge of energy at the start of a new role.

When you explode with joy as you share your ideas with those around you.

Mihaly Csikszentmihalyi calls this experience "flow."[1] It's a state of deep immersion, focus, and enjoyment where we are so absorbed in an activity that we lose track of time and operate at our best. Creativity feels effortless. Self-consciousness fades. The joy of co-creating with God becomes its own reward, independent of any external outcomes.

These times must be seized and savored for all they offer us. Because we know life isn't always like this. The long, dark stretch of winter is still fresh in our minds. That's why we must allow ourselves to open up the gates and run.

Creativity and Abundance

In the growing season, the focus for the vine is up and out. The flow is natural, organic, and exceedingly rapid. It is a vibrant invitation to simply participate in God's overflowing abundance.

Hildegard von Bingen calls this *viriditas*, or "the greening power of the Divine."[2] For her, *viriditas* was the very vitality of God pulsing through all creation. It is the creative force of the Spirit that animates, renews, and brings all things to life in the natural and spiritual realms.

---

1. Mihaly Csikszentmihalyi, *Flow: The Psychology of Optimal Experience* (New York: HarperPerennial, 1990).

2. Hildegard von Bingen, *Scivias*, trans. Mother Columba Hart (New York: Paulist Press, 1990), 52.

When the Spirit hovers over creation, something new emerges, multiplying and bursting forth in wondrous, diverse forms. Consider the Spirit's flow in Scripture:

- In Genesis 1, the Spirit hovers over creation, and with a word, new creation springs forth in all its wide variety. In Ellicott's commentary on Genesis, the Hebrew word for "hover" is described as "fluttered lovingly," conveying a loving energy that tenderly calls forth the latent possibilities of a budding world.[3]

- At the start of Jesus' ministry, the Spirit rests upon him like a dove at his baptism. This sets off the explosive growth of his ministry that would teach, heal, and deliver thousands.

- In Acts 2, when the Holy Spirit rests upon the disciples at Pentecost, they are empowered with spiritual gifts to take risks, share the Gospel, heal, deliver, and teach. By the Spirit's power, the Lord daily adds to their community people from all tribes, nations, and cultures.

This creative profusion of life is seeded deep within creation's design. Think about it:

- Newborn females possess two million eggs already hidden away in their tiny bodies.

- Over a lifetime, a man will generate more than 500 billion sperm cells.

- Fruit trees produce far more fruit than is eaten each year.

---

3. Charles John Ellicott, *Ellicott's Commentary on the Whole Bible, Vol. 1: Genesis to 2 Samuel* (Grand Rapids: Zondervan, 2008).

❧ A single grapevine can produce up to 40 clusters of grapes in a season, far more than it can ripen.

What does this tell us about God?

It tells us that we serve a God of extravagant abundance. A God whose resources never deplete, whose creativity never dries up, whose love overflows in ways that exceed comprehension. This kind of exponential growth reveals the infinite Source who fuels it all.

These moments of rapid, Spirit-led expansion are not the result of human striving, but of divine overflow. They are unexplainable, mysterious, and cannot be controlled. The real work, then, is to participate in the Spirit's flow instead of resisting it. As Joseph Chilton Pearce says, "We must accept that this creative pulse within us is God's creative pulse itself."[4]

In the growing season, we become channels of that divine abundance—vessels for God's love and inspiration. Whatever your arena of creativity, the place your true self thrives, you need to know that there is a wellspring within you that is infinite. It is fueled by the boundless love of God that can never be tapped out, never run dry.

It's planting lettuce and watching it multiply faster than you can possibly eat.

It's generating so many ideas in the workplace that not all of them can be used.

It's coming up with multiple creative solutions to the same problem.

---

4. Joseph Chilton Pearce, *The Crack in the Cosmic Egg: New Constructs of Mind and Reality* (New York: Inner Traditions, 1992), 150.

It's generating millions of lines of code.

It's practicing a thousand different ways to love the people around you.

The Spirit is always hovering over you, yearning to creatively express his love through you in abundant, multiplicative ways beyond what you could ever imagine. So many more possibilities are available to you than you could ever even actualize in your lifetime.

This is the nature of divine creativity: it is limitless. And for that creativity to be released, it needs space—room to stretch and grow without constraint.

Unhindered Growth

As Dave explained, after bud break, the vine throws out branches without any concern for the fruit. Growth happens freely, unpressured by the need to ripen fruit. That part comes later.

But in *the Productivity-Driven Approach*, there's no room for this kind of freedom. When the focus is on outcomes, there's no margin for error. There's no time to explore. There's no room for failure, because if what matters is the end result, then it must be a success.

The Flourishing Approach, however, is different. It makes space for generosity, openness, and playfulness. There's space to take risks, try new things, even fail, because in this paradigm, failure isn't the end. It's part of our formation. It teaches us which branches to keep and which to release.

At the heart of this distinction lies the difference between producing and creating:

- Producing is externally driven by outcomes, efficiency, and metrics.

- Creating flows from within, rooted in presence, play, and participation with the Spirit.

Could we allow ourselves grow like the vine after bud break—wild and free, without the pressure to produce?

What if we released the need to prove ourselves, and simply surrendered to the creative process?

What if we let go of the outcome and instead trusted its origin?

What might emerge if we trusted the infinite Source within—the one who invites us to experiment, to explore, to risk, to play?

Real growth doesn't begin with striving. It begins with surrender:
Surrender of outcomes.
Surrender of the opinions of others.
Surrender to the voice within.
Surrender to the Spirit flowing through our unique design.

True creativity is not born from control, but from trust. The vine doesn't force fruit into being; it simply yields to become what it already is.

John O'Donohue says it well:

> When we are creative, we help the unknown become known, the visible to be seen, and the rich darkness within us to become illuminated. .... Each of us is emerging at every moment. ... When we discover our creativity, we begin to attend to the constant emergence of who we are.[5]

---

5. O'Donohue, *Beauty*, 92.

The Ugly Phase

For a long time before my sabbatical, the pressure to produce "good" work kept me from creating. When I was focused on the outcome and getting it "right," it kept me from taking risks because I was afraid of failing. But, when I freed myself up to just enjoy the process without worrying about the result, I found myself connecting more deeply with God and allowing his creativity to flow through me.

I rediscovered joy in risk. In trying new things. In embracing the unknown. I learned that creating required generosity: generosity with my time, my attempts, and my experiments.

Which also meant creating a lot of ugly art.

The reality is, when the creative life force of the Spirit is channeled in and through us, it comes in fits and starts. It doesn't come out perfectly in fine lines of calligraphy that twist into delicate strokes. No, it comes in a wild, unruly, and often confusing mess that gets tangled and intertwined like the branches of the vine.

If you are a writer or artist of any kind, you know that sometimes it takes thousands of gallons of paint to understand the shape a piece is taking. Sometimes you must go through miles of pages just to find out what the story is about. Instead of seeing this as a waste or a sign of failure, could we reframe it like Thomas Edison did and simply acknowledge that sometimes it takes 10,000 attempts to create a light bulb?

Don't let the fear of failure or waste stop you. Don't let it keep you from opening yourself to the creative force within. Much of the time, it is cleaning you out as it goes, like running water through a drain that has been clogged for months and has finally broken free.

Like the sap flowing up through the vine, the means, methods, and direction our work takes is an expression of the source from the roots. And for us, the source is love. It pours out in wild wonder as a generous gift, an overflowing offering to those around us, transforming us as it goes.

As Brenda Ueland writes, "Why should we all use our creative power...? Because there is nothing that makes people so generous, joyful, lively, bold and compassionate, so indifferent to fighting and the accumulation of objects and money."[6]

Now here's where we must pause and mark a shift:
After that wild, generative creative phase comes careful cultivation. When the vine has had a chance to explode into multiple branches, the vinedresser refines what has grown through cultural practices like:

- **Suckering:** removing unwanted shoots that drain the vine's energy.

- **Tucking:** guiding early shoots into neat rows along the trellis, with the fruiting zone clearly positioned along the main canes.

- **Trimming and Thinning:** cutting back excess leaves and shoots to maximize sunlight and allow airflow, preventing mildew and disease.

For the vine, this is called "canopy management." And the purpose? Not to suppress growth, but to *focus it.*

---

6. Brenda Ueland, *If You Want to Write: A Book about Art, Independence and Spirit* (Minneapolis: Graywolf Press, 2007), 43.

Canopy Management

Canopy management ensures the vine continues to channel its energy into the most essential branches. It keeps the vine organized, balanced, and open—allowing light and air to reach what needs to grow.

Dave explained it this way:

> The vine is trying to be as vigorous as possible. Even though we pruned it, it's still going to throw out more branches than we need. I'm going to take shoots off to clear up any confusion about where the fruit will be. The vine doesn't know we're making wine, so I'm going to take off all the growth that doesn't matter to help it focus on the buds that *do* matter for fruit-bearing. It's a refocusing of the vine.

This is the editing process. It's the phase where we step back and ask:

- What is essential?

- What needs to be cut back?

- What needs to be trained in a clearer direction?

Unlike the experimental stage, where growth can go any which way, this is about refining and realigning that growth in the right direction. Canopy management isn't in contradiction to the creative flow—it's the complement.

There is a time to explore, to experiment, to grow wildly.
And there is a time to refine.

There is a time to try everything.
And there is a time to focus.

There is a time for playful, chaotic growth.
And there is a time for order.

Without discernment, creative energy can scatter. Mission drift, the gradual deviation from one's original purpose, is a real thing. We see it happen when a clear beginning slowly gets diluted by competing priorities or outside pressures.

Like vines, we are easily distracted. We tend to respond most quickly to the loudest external stimuli: emails, social media, the news, and the needs of family and friends. It all calls us to respond.

But, if we answer every call, we end up fragmented. We may have emerged from dormancy with clarity and conviction, but when our energy and attention is divided, our resources run thin and the quality of what we offer suffers.

I can't give my kids the attention they deserve while responding to work emails.
I can't give a project the excellence it needs while juggling six others.
I may be growing, but not fruitfully. Not intentionally. Not in the way that produces fruit that lasts.

In this way, canopy management becomes a spiritual practice of discernment to let go of what doesn't matter to make room for what truly does.

Essentialism

Greg McKeown describes this discernment process as essentialism. He puts it this way:

> Essentialism is not about how to get more things done; it's about how to get the right things done. ... It is about making the wisest possible investment of your time and energy

in order to operate at our highest point of contribution by doing only what is essential.[7]

The good news is, this work isn't all on us. God isn't distant, waiting for us to get it right. He gently tends to the branches of the vine, saying, *"Let's look at this together."*

Just as the vinedresser removes unnecessary leaves and branches, when we allow God to cut away the distractions that are siphoning our energy, we can focus on our most valuable contributions to his kingdom.

The question is: Do we make it a point to regularly ask him?

- Where am I drifting?

- What needs to go?

- What's the "main thing" you're asking me to grow right now?

- Is my growth organized in the right direction?

- Are my actions aligned with my values? With *your* values?

- Is there enough space in my life for the light and movement of the Spirit to flow through?

This discernment process is rarely a solitary endeavor. It requires the insight and support of those who love us. When we engage this process in community, we gain clarity through diverse perspectives and collective wisdom. Community offers accountability, encouragement, and guidance to help us stay aligned with kingdom values.

---

7. Greg McKeown, *Essentialism: The Disciplined Pursuit of Less* (New York: Crown Business, 2014), 5.

Community and Aligning with Our Values

A few years into my time with *Boundless*, I stepped into leading our online prayer days. Around the same time, our team went through a difficult transition. The demands were so intense that I could barely keep up with the communication and responsibilities required to manage it all.

Right when I was hitting a breaking point, I had a check-in with Ang, one of the leaders of *Boundless* and my support in this role. As we talked through the expectations I had been placing on myself, it became clear to Ang that they were far higher than she had imagined and wildly unrealistic. With compassion in her voice, she said, "Of course you're overwhelmed and burning out!"

She then began naming practical ways we could lighten the load by cutting responsibilities and streamlining communication to reduce the pressure I was under.

At that moment, I was walking on my treadmill (a typical achiever move) during our Zoom call. Ang named the concern she had for what the current workload was doing to my emotional health and stress level. Then she said, "I would much rather cut some projects than hold up the current system that is burning you out."

All of a sudden, I had to stop walking. I straddled the sides of the treadmill, and braced myself against the desk, blinking back tears.

"What are these tears, Bette?" Ang asked gently.

Swallowing hard, I wiped the tears away. My throat tightened as I grasped for an explanation, "I'm just not used to this. Usually, when a project is threatened, the expectation is that I have to push through to make it happen, no matter the cost. I'm not used to someone choosing my thriving over a project's success."

When I said this, this admission caught both of us by surprise. I was so used to just wearing myself out in the name of progress that I didn't know what it would be like to let go of an outcome and choose my health instead. I had formed my entire organizational identity around my ability to get things done, even at the expense of my stress level and relationships. This was a completely new value system.

Choosing Thriving over Output

As we both grappled with these shifts grounded in *the Flourishing Approach*, Ang suggested several things we could cut back to refocus my energy into the most important things. She shared, "We could limit the size of your team. We could choose to not do prayer day for July and allow you to focus on the new team members. This would free you up to build into these relationships without the expectations of a project."

Each of these suggestions felt entirely countercultural. And yet, they were deeply aligned with the flourishing mindset of the kingdom, where the focus is on people over projects.

Together, we invited the Vinedresser to sucker away unnecessary shoots—those seemingly good, but ultimately distracting expenditures of energy. It was painful to let go of these things, especially when I had such high expectations of myself to do it all. And yet, when I allowed God to clip them away, I felt an unexpected relief. With fewer outputs, I could focus on what would ultimately bear the fruit of the kingdom.

When we yield to the Spirit's leadership in community, our priorities shift. This kind of canopy management creates space for shared thriving—where the community of branches ripens the best kind of fruit together.

Digging Deeper:

1. Where have you found yourself most often in a "flow" state?

2. Where is God inviting you to just focus on growing instead of fruit right now?

3. Where might God want to "refocus" your energy into your most essential contribution to the kingdom?

Chapter 12:

Flowering

The July air radiates with humidity as Dave and I weave our way through a row of Chardonnay vines at Ten Hands Vineyard. They have reached for the sky, arms flung wide along the trellis, pulsing with life. Just weeks ago, Dave carefully suckered the wild shoots and gently guided the growth so the branches could rise in clean lines toward the top wire.

As we reach the center of the row, he pauses. "Do you smell that?" he asks. I take a deep breath, and a warm, sweet fragrance alights on me, permeating the humid air and wrapping around us like a cloak. I look down toward the fruiting zone and see the tiny flowers shyly make their appearance like miniature white sparklers. Here in Northern Michigan, they explode in a silent spectacle around the Fourth of July. The petals are so small you have to get close to see them jutting out from the green clusters, which look like tiny grapes.

Dave pulls a cluster of flowers from the vine and cradles it in his palm. It spreads out over half of his hand in a fuzzy, cone-like shape with soft, thin petals jutting out from all sides. As he gently brushes his fingers along the petals, they fall off like confetti. These blossoms are fragile, vulnerable to wind, rain, and frost.

Flowering lasts just one to two weeks, and Dave tells me he hopes for dry, sunny weather, so nothing can disrupt the polli-nation process. Because in this tender, short window, the vine opens itself to give and receive from its neighboring branches. As it does, it reveals its most hidden and inner beauty: delicate petals that fill the vineyard with a sweet fragrance. Once polli-nated, the blossoms quickly wither, their beauty giving way for something more enduring: the slow ripening of grapes.

What often goes unnoticed in this brief scene is that the flower does not set fruit by itself, but through an invisible exchange between distinct parts of the vine. Carried by the wind, bees, or simple proximity, it is a quiet act of communion in diversity. Flowering is not only a display of beauty, but an act of interdependence.

Fruitfulness is born through the courageous and beautiful act of mutual vulnerability. As philosopher Schopenhauer writes, "Opposites throw light upon each other. Beauty does not belong exclusively to the regions of light and loveliness, cut off from the conversation of oppositions. The vigour and vitality of beauty derives precisely from the heart of difference."[1]

---

1. O'Donohue, *Beauty*, 40, quoting Schopenhauer.

The Flower Sets the Fruit

In Genesis, when God says, "Be fruitful and multiply,"[2] he issues what theologians call the *cultural mandate*. God separates, then he brings together. New creation emerges when difference comes together in union, sparking the multiplication of life that fills the world with his glory.

But this fruitfulness extends beyond physical union between man and woman. In Christ, the multiplication of the kingdom unfolds through the diverse, Spirit-filled community of the church. Jesus fulfills and reframes "be fruitful and multiply" when he commissions his disciples: "Go and make disciples of all nations."[3] In the Great Commission, instead of physical offspring spreading across the earth, it is a spiritual family, born of the Spirit and propagated through love.

At Pentecost, when the Spirit descended upon the disciples, it was like the blossoming of the vine. God's beauty unfolded in a chorus of diverse tongues, much like flowers blooming across the vineyard—each one unique, yet part of a shared act of pollination and connection. In this miraculous moment, people from every nation were drawn together, and something entirely new was born.

Theologian Willie Jennings captures this scene beautifully in his commentary on Acts:

"The Spirit creates joining. The followers of Jesus are now being connected in a way that joins them to people in the most intimate space—of voice, memory, sound, body, land, and place."[4]

---

2. Genesis 1:28.

3. Matthew 28:19.

4. Willie Jennings, *Acts: A Theological Commentary on the Bible* (Louisville: Westminster John Knox Press, 2017), 28.

This act of joining—the communion among body of Christ—is the flowering that precedes the kingdom's fruit. From the Spirit, a variety of gifts emerge, drawing us into interdependence, where unity is not the erasure of difference, but the beauty formed through it.

As Paul writes in Ephesians 4:11–13:

> So Christ himself gave the apostles, the prophets, the evangelists, the pastors and teachers, to equip his people for works of service, so that the body of Christ may be built up until we all reach unity in the faith and in the knowledge of the Son of God and become mature, attaining to the whole measure of the fullness of Christ.

Beholding Beauty

The flowers on a vine can only fulfill their purpose when they are properly received by one another. Pollen needs space, time, and proximity to sink deeply into neighboring blossoms, sparking an unseen transformation. Likewise, just as the flowering stage is essential for fruit to form, so too is a season of mutual openness essential for the formation of kingdom fruit.

It doesn't have to be a long season, but it does require intentionality. We must cultivate hospitable spaces where we can see and be seen, where we are free to unfold vulnerably in the gaze of others and to behold one another with reverence. These moments are like walking through a vineyard in full bloom. As we take in the beauty of each other's presence, we are stirred with delight by the image of God reflected in our midst.

The invitation, then, is to receive one another as the flowering vines do—held in the long gaze of the summer sun. This kind of communion is marked by joy, laughter, awe, and wonder. When we slow down long enough to truly see others, not for what they produce, but for who they are, we are on our way to ripening good fruit.

And yet, in communities shaped by *the Productivity-Driven Approach*, this flowering stage is often overlooked or rushed. Rarely do we pause long enough to truly see and celebrate the sacred presence of those in our midst. Too often, our relationships are formed around what we hope to accomplish, rather than our shared humanity. In our utility-driven culture, prioritizing connection can feel inefficient, even indulgent.

But in God's design, flowering always precedes fruit. As we behold one another's unique voice and allow different perspectives to shape us, new and beautiful things emerge. We cross-pollinate through the exchange of stories, dreams, and presence—and from that shared vulnerability, new creation is born.

It's the moment someone risks sharing a half-formed idea, and another person says, *"That stirs something in me ..."*

It's when a different perspective is offered in a meeting, and we pause long enough to let it shift our direction.

It's the church potluck where we savor dishes from a variety of traditions.

> It's when we allow those different from
> us to speak into our lives to offer wisdom,
> encouragement, or exhortation.

Flowering in Community

There's something sacred that happens when we are seen and welcomed. For me, as both an artist and a woman in ministry, it has taken time to find spaces where my voice isn't merely tolerated, but celebrated. Yet, when it happens, something begins to bloom. Life is sparked—not just in me, but in the communities I belong to.

When I joined *Boundless*, I was struck by the beauty of its initiatives and the leaders behind them. Each carry a unique expression of healing, justice, and restoration into the world. While inspired, I also found myself wondering what I, as an artist, had to offer.

Then, Danielle invited me to create a painting for IMBY (In My Back Yard), the initiative that builds tiny homes for those at risk of homelessness. She asked if I could create a piece that could be printed and installed in each new IMBY build as a visual reminder of home and belonging to the new residents.

As I prayed about what to create, I saw an image of a mother bird tending her eggs in a nest. Psalm 84:3 came to mind:

"Even the sparrow has found a home,
and the swallow a nest for herself,
where she may have her young—
a place near your altar."

I envisioned a sanctuary of belonging—a nest hidden and safe in God's presence, a place for new beginnings.

Later, I learned that when the founders were discerning IMBY's vision, they attended a prayer gathering to seek God's perspective. Without knowing their plans, the woman who prayed over them said, "I see an image of a tree with birds in a nest and a fox hole at the bottom. It reminds me of the passage where Jesus says, 'Foxes have holes and birds have nests, but the Son of Man has no place to lay his head.' I think you're going to build homes for Jesus."

And that's exactly what they're doing. In building homes for the vulnerable, they are building homes for Jesus, who said: "Truly I tell you, whatever you did for one of the least of these brothers and sisters of mine, you did for me."[5]

Before knowing any of this, I created a painting of a mother swallow hovering over her baby chicks and titled it, *Home*. Last year, I had the joy of delivering a print to the first completed IMBY build and celebrating the beauty of what their team had created.

Like a flower opening to receive pollen from neighboring branches, the more I have opened myself to the IMBY founders and their dreams, the more I have been inspired. And as they welcome my gifts to the table, I too open like a blossom in the sunlight, offering something in return. Together, through this mutual exchange, it ripens something new.

The flowering didn't stop at the creation of the *Home* painting. It continues every time I share it with others and invite them to reflect. A few months after finishing the painting, I brought it to

---

5. Matthew 25:40.

Toronto to give to the IMBY founders. I led their team in a prayer practice called *visio divina*, Latin for "divine seeing." It's a way of praying with visual art. What followed was a beautiful tapestry of insight and story sparked by the image.

Danielle later shared:

> Our ragtag crew of misfits related to the vulnerability of the little bird. The feeling of just awakening to a new way of living and needing help to do it. We also saw ourselves in the strength, protection, and provision of the mother bird who is showing up. We saw the possibilities of the eggs not yet hatched. The awakenings to come. The gold background reminded us that everything we do and are becoming is laced with sacredness.

It was a moment of cross-pollination. The painting, born from their vision, returned to them as encouragement—a visual reminder of their call. This is mutuality: when we bring our gifts and receive the gifts of others, something generative happens. Like pollination that sets the fruit, this exchange becomes the very act through which the kingdom grows.

Mutuality

The beauty of the flowering process lies in its mutuality. Pollination depends on a sacred exchange; each flower must both give and receive. Fruit cannot form if a flower only offers pollen without accepting it, nor can it grow if it only receives but does not give. Interdependence and reciprocity pulse through the veins of creation.

We've all experienced one-sided relationships. Perhaps we've felt the weight of constantly giving support, wisdom, or resources with little in return. Or maybe we've been on the receiving end, stuck in a cycle of need. While some imbalance is natural in relationships like mentor and mentee or parent and child, true partnership in advancing the kingdom calls for reciprocity. When it's absent, both parties suffer: the giver adopts a prideful savior-like posture, while the receiver feels dehumanized, trapped in perpetual dependence.

But mutuality affirms our shared humanity. Each person has value to offer, especially those who are different from us. If we want to create a flourishing vineyard, it means creating a culture where every gift, background, ethnicity, and gender is honored, celebrated, and contributes to our collective growth.

Gisela Kreglinger says it well:

> When the unity of the church is reduced to homogeneity of opinions and habits, stages in life, economic status, or educational background, then the vital flourishing of life in the Christian sense is more difficult ... we must learn, like the vintner-craftsman, to see diversity as a gift rather than a threat. It enriches our understanding of God as our Creator and challenges us to trust that God's love and grace work to redeem us precisely in those differences and the challenges that they bring.[6]

It is this kind of urgency that must drive the church. Because if we don't see, celebrate, honor, and welcome those different from us, we literally cannot bear fruit. And yet, the opposite is what we often witness in the Western church. We have become

---

6. Gisela Kreglinger, *The Spirituality of Wine*, (Grand Rapids: Eerdmans, 2016), 207.

increasingly polarized, separated along ethnic, cultural, political, and theological lines. Sunday morning remains one of the most segregated hours of the week.[7]

Even in our attempts to move toward diversity, we often create diverse platforms to honor the appearance of inclusion, but we don't really welcome these voices to shape the culture or systems we are in. There's a vast difference between offering someone a seat at the table and beholding them in a way that transforms us and the entire structure of our organizations.

For those of us in majority culture, this requires humility and intentionality. We must resist the urge to center our own perspectives or mold others into our existing frameworks. True mutuality isn't about simply making space for diverse voices, it's about shared agency. It asks us to move beyond inclusion toward transformation, especially by entrusting leadership to those who have long been excluded.

This kind of reciprocity has the power to heal the entire vineyard community. But, it begins when we recognize that we cannot flourish without one another. The presence, perspectives, and gifts of those different from us are not optional, they are essential. Without them, we will rot on the vine.

As Lilla Watson, an Indigenous Australian from the Gangulu Nation, once said:

---

7. Martin Luther King Jr., "Can a Christian Be a Communist?" sermon delivered at Ebenezer Baptist Church, Atlanta, GA, September 30, 1962, *The Martin Luther King, Jr. Papers Project*, Stanford University, https://kinginstitute.stanford.edu/king-papers/documents/can-christian-be-communist.

"If you have come here to help me, you are wasting your time. But if you have come because your liberation is bound up with mine, then let us work together."[8]

The Biodiversity of the Kingdom

This sacred reciprocity doesn't just appear in the flowering stage of the vine, it pulses throughout the entire ecosystem, from composting and cover cropping to the diverse life cultivated on the land. The vineyard teaches us: diversity is not merely aesthetic, it is essential to survival.

Dave explains, "There's nothing that kills the health of a vineyard faster than a monoculture." He illustrates this through composting: "If you want to add health, quality, and vitality to the soil, good compost is the best and fastest way. One tablespoon of compost can contain thousands of different species of living microorganisms. The more variety and diversity in the soil and plants on the farm, the better."

When a vineyard is cultivated with biodiversity—through intercropping and symbiotic relationships among plants and animals—life flourishes. Organic matter increases, nutrients replenish, and erosion is reduced. The result is a more sustainable, resilient, and fruitful ecosystem.

As Kreglinger observes, "Surely, the wine that comes forth from such a vineyard is richer, more complex, and inspiring to a world

---

8. Quote attributed to Aboriginal activists group, often associated with Lilla Watson, an Indigenous Australian from the Gangulu Nation. Watson has stated that the quote emerged from a collective of Aboriginal activists in Queensland in the 1970s.

that suffers from increasing homogenization, on the one hand, and fragmentation, alienation, and isolation on the other."[9]

Yet since the Industrial Revolution, many farms have shifted toward monocultures for the sake of efficiency and short-term gains. This *Productivity-Driven Approach* comes at a steep cost: depleted soil, carbon loss, increased erosion, and greater vulnerability to disease—all threatening long-term sustainability.[10]

What's true of vineyards is true of human communities. The most fruitful ones embrace the complexity of their terroir: the diversity of gifts, cultures, experiences, and voices that shape a people.

Even the metrics prized by *the Productivity-Driven Approach* affirm this: a 2015 McKinsey & Company study found that companies in the top quartile for racial and ethnic diversity were 35% more likely to outperform their peers in profitability. Teams with gender-diverse leadership were 15% more likely to achieve above-average returns.[11]

These findings underscore the creative and strategic power of diversity. When teams come together across a variety of backgrounds and perspectives, they explore a broader range of ideas, make stronger decisions, and innovate more effectively.

God has designed us to thrive within an interwoven web of voices, cultures, genders, and perspectives. But this kind of ecosystem doesn't grow by accident. It requires partnering with

---

9. Kreglinger, *The Spirituality of Wine*, 207.

10. Chris Kresser. "Depletion of Soil and What Can Be Done." *Chris Kresser.* Accessed September 18, 2024, https://chriskresser.com/depletion-of-soil-and-what-can-be-done/.

11. McKinsey & Company. "Why Diversity Matters." January 2015. Accessed September 2023, https://www.mckinsey.com/business-functions/organization/our-insights/why-diversity-matters.

the Vinedresser to cultivate connection, interdependence, and shared purpose. Without intentional belonging across differences, there is no lasting fruit. Yet when people of varied backgrounds and experiences come together within the body of Christ, new life emerges—new ideas, new dreams, and fresh vitality that multiplies the fruit of the kingdom.

Digging Deeper:

1. How have you experienced "flowering" and mutuality in your community?

2. What are ways you've seen diversity create better quality fruit?

3. What has been difficult or costly about practicing mutuality across differences? What fears, habits, or assumptions have you had to unlearn in order to truly receive from someone unlike you?

Part IV:
The Life of Christ

RESURRECTION
Ascent into the Branches
BUD BREAK – GROWING – FLOWERING

LIFE
Ripening Fruit
VERAISON – HARVEST – WINE

PRUNING – DORMANCY – POST-HARVEST
Descent into the Roots
DEATH

Chapter 13:

Ripening Fruit

It's early August when Dave and I visit the Pinot Gris vines at Brigadoon Lane Vineyard in Suttons Bay. The leaves have flattened and broadened out over the last several months, deepening from sage to forest green. I lift a few leaves from the canopy to take a closer look at the fruiting zone near where the vine is tied to the trellis.

Miniature clusters of grapes shoot out sideways from the branches, alert and happy. The pollinated flowers have done their job, and the fruit has emerged from where the delicate petals once were a month ago. I squeeze a few of the grapes gently with my fingers and they are as firm as apples. The grapes themselves are a lime green no larger than the size of pencil erasers. Over the next few months, they will grow to the size of marbles, softening and deepening in color.

Dave gets down on one knee and assesses the fruiting zone. He says, "When the vine is in the growing season between bud break and flowering, it's throwing out leaves everywhere because it is just trying to focus on growth. But, when the fruit is set after flowering, the vine shifts its energy from growing branches to ripening fruit."

Ultimately, this shift marks the vine's transition from simply *growing for itself to giving itself away*. The fruit becomes a gift, meant to nourish and bless in ways that multiply the seed it carries.

The Shift from Branches to Fruit

If abiding with Christ in his death roots us in **belovedness**, and abiding in his resurrection connects us into a sense of **belonging** among the branches, then abiding in his life bears the fruit of **blessing** others. This fruit is the gift of our lives—surrendered to God, formed in community, and poured out in love.

As we grow secure in our attachment to God and one another, our gaze begins to shift outward. We no longer need to cling to self-protection or self-promotion; we are already held and known. As we enter this phase of fruitfulness, we partner with God in his mission, allowing his love to ripen through us into a self-giving, sacrificial offering for the sake of the world.

Do you remember at the beginning of this book, when Dave told me that vinedressers don't pay much attention to the fruit? Instead, he said that good vinedressers pay attention to the health, quality, and vitality of the vine. If a vinedresser cultivates a vine toward flourishing, then quality fruit will follow.

Scripture uses the same imagery. According to the *Dictionary of Biblical Imagery*, the fruit of a harvest represents "the consummation of a process that must be worked out over time, like the full program of God's kingdom."[1]

The Fulfillment of Cultivation over Time

Dave says, "If you come to this season and have done the work in the growing months prior, you will look at the fruit and see that it is clean and happy. Now, it's just a matter of time before you can reap it. If there is a high level of observation and responsiveness to the vine during the growing season, then the investment made pays off in the fruit."

Good, lasting fruit ripens through seasons of abiding in the Vine and surrendering to the Vinedresser's faithful care. As Jesus said, "If you remain in me and I in you, you will bear much fruit; apart from me you can do nothing."[2]

Fruitfulness comes from remaining in Christ through every season as:

- We face our false selves and die to them through confession, lament, and repentance in post-harvest.

- We rest in silence, solitude, and stillness, and let new dreams awaken in the dormancy of winter.

- We let go of our own way and trust the Vinedresser's patient perspective in pruning.

- We courageously burst through resistance to offer our true selves at bud break.

---

1. Ryken, Wilhoit, and Longman, *Dictionary of Biblical Imagery*, 365.

2. John 15:5.

- We surrender to the creative process as resurrection life pulses through us during the growing season.

- We give and receive in mutuality, setting the fruit through flowering in the community of branches.

It is the culmination of all these moments of abiding that slowly ripens a harvest worth gathering.

So the question remains: What has been ripening in you through abiding in Jesus that is now ready to be given away?

Sometimes it is the gift of ourselves, but sometimes it is also the fruits of our hands—the result of our labor of love that grows out of a heart devoted to Jesus.

A Harvest Worth Waiting For

When my first book, *Making Room in Advent* arrived at my house, my husband, Steven, and I were just on our way out the door for a date night. It had been left on the doorstep and he noticed it while I was getting ready. As I came out of the bathroom and made my way to the door, I asked, "You ready?"

Steven leaned against the counter trying to suppress a smile as he casually shifted the box toward me and feigned indifference as he said, "Sure, I just thought maybe you might want to open this first."

I burst over to him and squealed, "It's here?!" gripping the box tightly in my hands. We brought the box out to the back porch and Steven filmed me while I frantically opened it, my whole body jumping up and down with excitement. As the box popped open, I quickly grabbed the book, held it in my hands and studied it, running my hand over the embossed cover and beaming ear to ear.

There was something so profoundly sacred for me in this moment. It wasn't just the book I held in my hands, but it was the fullness of something that had ripened over decades that made this moment so powerful. Like a vine that grew slowly through various seasons of life, death, and resurrection, deepening roots and surrendering to the cultivation of the Vinedresser, I had been on a lengthy journey to get to this point.

It was the moment in second grade when my teacher noticed all the drawings and stories I was writing in class and told me I could be an author and illustrator someday.

It was the thousands of hours in the studio or on the page to hone my craft, the countless ugly paintings and crappy first drafts to craft the right sentence or just the right shade of blue. It was the moments of wanting to throw paintings against the wall and the moments of mysterious breakthrough when the piece would reveal what it needed next.

It was the many years resisting my calling as an artist and trying to blend in, and then the courage to finally own it. It was the many friends, family members, and mentors who called this work out of me as they named the true artist-self within.

This book represented so much of who I had become as I yielded to the mysterious and winding progression of the work layer by layer, and word by word. My true self had been unfolding in profound intimacy with God in the creative process, ripening into the work itself.

As I stood there on my back porch beholding the book in my hands, I experienced an embodied encounter of harvest that filled me with such overflowing joy that I could not keep to myself. I could not wait to share this work with the world. And in that moment, I screamed aloud and then promptly posted about it on social media.

Sometimes we need palpable moments like this. Moments when we experience the physical culmination of the fruit worth celebrating. We experience these occasions in all kinds of ways in our lives:

- It's the birth of a child after seasons of infertility or loss.

- It's the acceptance letter to the school you had been preparing to get into.

- It's the celebrations of birthdays and graduations and weddings.

- It's the moment of baptism when your faith is made public.

- It's the celebration service of a life well lived.

These celebrations mark not only the moment themselves, but the deeply profound work God does within us as we abide in him and ripen fruit over time from our sacred attachment to the True Vine. Every stage of our lives contributes to a harvest—from the moment a dream is planted within us, to the long, slow, and meandering path to get there.

Fruit That Comes from Within

We may encounter harvest in tangible forms, such as a book held in our hands, or in ways that are harder to grasp. Regardless, as we've learned from Dave, fruit is not merely what appears on the outside; it represents what has been cultivated within, ultimately finding expression outwardly. This fruit reflects the health, quality, and vitality of the vine itself.

Jesus expressed this when he said, "You don't get wormy apples off a healthy tree, nor good apples off a diseased tree. The health of the apple tells the health of the tree. You must begin with your own life-giving lives. It's who you are, not what you say and do, that counts. Your true being brims over into true words and deeds."[3]

In God's economy, the harvest isn't always something "out there" in ways we can gather or quantify. Often, it's "in here," expressed as the overflow of who we are being cultivated to be, the flesh-and-blood presence of Jesus in the world.

As St. Teresa of Ávila writes,

Christ has no body but yours.
No hands, no feet on earth but yours,
Yours are the eyes with which he looks
Compassion on this world,
Yours are the feet with which he walks to do good,
Yours are the hands, with which He blesses all the world.[4]

We all have the honor of partnering with God to embody his love in deeply tangible ways.

> The fragrance of God's love drifts through the house with the warmth of freshly baked bread shared with dinner guests.
>
> The strength of God's love rises in the support beams of a tiny home built for those at risk of homelessness.
>
> The taste of God's love lingers in squash grown from a community garden, nourishing families who can't afford fresh produce.

---

3. Luke 6:43–45, MSG.

4. Teresa of Ávila, "Christ Has No Body," in *The Longing in Between: Sacred Poetry from Around the World*, ed. Ivan M. Granger (Louisville, CO: Poetry Chaikhana Press, 2014), 89.

The warmth of God's love wraps around someone who is grieving through the embrace of a friend.

The sound of God's love resonates in the attentive silence of someone listening deeply to another's story.

Like the vine that delicately weaves the energy of the sun into sweet grapes, we embody the love of God into every act of kindness, creativity, and sacrifice. The harvest is an outpouring of all God's good and heavenly gifts through flesh and blood people like you and me. And that kind of harvest reproduces for eternity.

The Seeds of the Kingdom

In October, as Dave and I walk among the Chardonnay vines at Ten Hands Vineyard during harvest, he tells me what he's been up to while the grapes have been ripening. "I've been out here every couple of days," he says, "tasting the fruit, watching for physiological ripeness—when the seeds turn from green to brown and the skin slips easily from the flesh."

He plucks a Riesling grape, squeezes it, and shows me how the seed pushes out from the green pulp. Then he hands me one. "Bite into it. See how it crunches in your mouth? The seed is ready, and now it is time to harvest."

The time for harvest is determined by the maturity of the seeds.

The purpose of fruit extends beyond the enjoyment and nourishment of the eater. It also facilitates *the propagation of its seeds.*

Fruit shelters the seed until it ripens, then releases it to return to the soil, often through digestion and scattering.

But here's something fascinating: grapes, like apples, are not "true to seed." That means if a grape seed falls to the ground and grows, it will not replicate the original grape. The new fruit will be genetically different, unique, and unpredictable.

As we discussed in Chapter 3, if vintners want to reproduce the exact same grape, they don't plant seeds. Instead, they take a cutting from the parent vine and graft it onto another rootstock. This ensures the new branch produces its same distinct fruit.

What a beautiful picture of spiritual formation.

When a branch is grafted onto the vine, it retains its unique shape, character, and distinct expression. The rootstock gives it a home, and supplies the new branch the life and resources it needs to grow and thrive in a new context. This is our relationship to the True Vine, as we discussed in Chapter 3. Wherever we are planted, we can thrive and produce the unique fruit we were created to bear when we are grafted onto the True Vine.

Yet, when fruit is pollinated through flowering, like we talked about in the last chapter, something new is born out of diversity and union. Fruit that comes from this process doesn't look or taste identical to the branch it comes from. It is a fresh expression. This is the way God's kingdom grows: not through replication, but through Spirit-led, diverse, and surprising new life. Remember, God's kingdom is not a monoculture. It is a wild vineyard of varied fruit expressed through different lives, cultures, and terroir.

Seeds and the Growth of the Kingdom

Jesus frequently employed seed imagery to illustrate how the kingdom grows. In Mark 4, he says the seed is the Word (v. 14), and later that the kingdom itself is like a farmer scattering seed (v. 26–32).

But here's a foundational truth about all seed-bearing fruit: the seed must be encased in something desirable. The more delicious and appealing the fruit, the more likely it is to be consumed, and in turn, the greater chance the seed will be spread and multiplied.

The same principle applies in winemaking. The quality of the fruit and the maturity of the seed directly impact its ability to become something greater than itself: a beautiful, unique, and enduring wine.

So, let's sit with this for a moment.

The vessel of the seed matters.

Have you ever bitten into a rotten piece of fruit and immediately spit it out? Me too. Many people today, especially the younger generation, are spitting out the fruit of the Western church. We may carry the seeds of God's Word and kingdom, but *how* we carry them matters. The fruit must reflect the character of Christ if it's going to carry his life forward.

A recent Barna study found that 27% of U.S. adults doubt the Christian faith due to negative experiences with religious institutions.[5] For the unchurched, the top reason for skepticism is the

---

5. Barna Group, *Doubt & Faith: Top Reasons People Question Christianity* (Ventura, CA: Barna Group, 2017), accessed October 30, 2024, https://www.barna.com/research/doubt-faith/.

"hypocrisy of religious people." Many who are reluctant to affiliate with a church say: "Christians seem closed and judgmental."

Rhett McLaughlin articulates this heartbreakingly well on the *Ear Biscuits* podcast:

> I say this out of love and respect because I do believe there is hope for the church. Kids are not leaving the church because you didn't train them enough. They're leaving the church because you trained them enough to develop a sense for truth and justice. You let them read the words of Jesus. And they got it. And they've recognized that the church doesn't seem to be interested in those words. They're not leaving because they don't know the truth, they're leaving because they do. ... If kids can't find the Jesus they know from the Bible that you've taught them about within the walls of your church, they will go looking for him elsewhere.[6]

Considering this, we must ask ourselves: What kind of fruit are we producing?

Do our lives reflect Jesus and the fruit of the Spirit? Or do they mirror the works of the flesh—what Paul warns against in Galatians 5:19–21: sexual immorality, idolatry, hatred, discord, jealousy, rage, selfish ambition, dissension, and division?

Given the church's reputation for hypocrisy, judgment, sexual abuse scandals, polarization, and idolatry, it's no wonder people are rejecting its fruit. But what if we offered something different? Fruit that was beautiful, nourishing, and life-giving? What if we

---

6. Rhett McLaughlin, "Rhett's Spiritual Deconstruction," *Ear Biscuits*, YouTube video, 1:49:29, posted by "Rhett & Link," February 9, 2020, https://www.youtube.com/watch?v=CnYG6x-aOTk.

bore fruit that tasted like Jesus—fruit worthy of carrying the seeds of the kingdom?

Paul encourages this very thing in Philippians 1:11 (MSG):

"Live a lover's life, circumspect and exemplary, a life Jesus will be proud of: bountiful in fruits from the soul, making Jesus Christ attractive to all, getting everyone involved in the glory and praise of God."

So, it begs the question:

Are we living a lover's life? A life that makes Jesus attractive to all?

Because the seed may be eternal, but the fruit that carries it? That's what the world will taste first. Let it be sweet and worthy of the harvest.

Digging Deeper:

1. The vine's shift from growing branches to ripening fruit parallels the transition from self-preservation to self-giving. How do you relate to this shift in your own life?

2. What are some fruits that have been ripening in you through many seasons of abiding in Jesus?

3. The vessel of the seed matters—how we embody the message of the kingdom matters. What do you think the fruit of your faith community tastes like? Does it reflect the character of Jesus? Why or why not?

Notes

Chapter 14:

Veraison

The sky is grey and heavy with rain clouds as I make my way up to Ed and Adina's vineyard in Suttons Bay in early September. Huddled under my raincoat, I walk through the light rain to the vineyard's south end, where Dave is assessing the same Pinot Gris vines we pruned together in April.

As we move deeper into the vineyard, a Starling distress call echoes from speakers on several trellis posts. Dave pulls back the bird netting to reveal grape clusters in the fruiting zone, now in veraison, or ripening. The clusters are a patchwork of green and purple.

"During veraison," Dave explains, "the ease of growing branches and leaves gives way to the strain of ripening fruit. What was once green turns red (or gray or yellow depending on the vine), and the grapes soften and sweeten."

To protect the ripening fruit, Ed, Adina, and Dave have taken several precautions. They've draped bird netting over the vines to keep birds from eating the grapes, and the distressed Starling cries discourage birds from landing. "We're trying to keep the birds from getting to the fruit before we're ready to harvest," Dave tells me.

Other threats, like black rot and mildew, also endanger the fruit. Dave explains,

> There are many things that can affect the grape clusters, but that's why we prepare. That's why we compost. When you strengthen the vine from the roots and care for the soil, the vine is naturally more resilient. If you focus only on outward signs of fruit and neglect the roots, you'll be in trouble when threats come.

Threats to the Fruit

As we start to ripen the fruit of God's kingdom, there is real resistance in the world to bearing this fruit, and the threats increase the closer we get to harvest. The evil one comes to steal, kill, and destroy,[1] like a cunning and ravenous fox that tramples through the vineyard, crushing its fruit. He comes with lies about our identity, seeking to prevent us from ripening into the fullness of who we were created to be, individually and collectively.

---

1. John 10:10.

As I begin to ripen the fruit of my creative work, one of the enemy's most persistent tactics is to make me doubt my calling, sowing seeds of guilt and shame for not doing enough for the vulnerable. The enemy taunts, "Look at all the suffering, poverty, and oppression in the world. Why aren't you doing more for the poor and marginalized? You're not doing enough."

If I am not vigilant to combat it, this lie continues to seep in, wrapping its tendrils around my heart and draining the life and joy out of the creative work. In my weaker moments when I give into this lie, I get depressed or get really busy making things happen through activism.

On my better days, when I draw from the deep roots of God's love, I simply reply, "You're right—I'm not enough. I'll never be enough to make even a small dent in healing the world's suffering. But this is the work God has called me to, and I trust that he will use it to advance his kingdom, even if I can't yet see how. So, you'll have to take it up with him."

To keep creating, I have to make it a regular practice to confront those lies with truth. If I don't, the work will never be created. When the work is still in progress, I can't rely on the endorphin hits of likes, shares, or even powerful testimonies of God moving through it. Instead, I have to draw from the roots of my divine identity and find joy in the process of doing what I alone was created to do.

Like Dave says about the vines, if we have a strong root system, if we are healthy and whole and know who we are, anchored in Christ's love as his beloved and know our belonging in the community of branches, we will be stronger and more resilient against the evil one's schemes. We will be able to stand our ground and say, "no," to the evil one amid the conflicts we face. The difference in the outcome to this resistance is whether or not we have prepared well to withstand the threats.

As the fruit ripens, we can also take steps to protect it like the bird netting and the Starling cries. Recently, as I was finishing up this book and preparing for several speaking engagements, I was reminded of this and thought, "if I don't get some bird netting to protect that fruit, it's going to get picked away." It was then that I reached out to my prayer team to cover my family and my creative work from the threats of the evil one.

As we think about the fruit ripening in our own lives, what can we do to protect it? What proactive steps can we take to safeguard the fruit as it matures?

The Stress of Ripening

Veraison is a point of conflict and stress after the fruit is set. As Dave says, "It's the most astringent point of the vine's life cycle. As the ripening process turns acidic and tart grapes sweet, it's like the end of a race. The vines are exhausted, but they are straining their remaining energy toward the finish line."

In some vineyards, vinedressers will intentionally "stress" the vines by withholding resources like water. The induced stress of limiting water, for example, forces the vines to dig their roots deeper, which creates a more complex, rich flavor in the wine.

Steve Smith, a wine and vine conductor at Smith & Sheth and Pyramid Valley in New Zealand described the process this way:

> Let's think like a vine ... if life is too easy, in fertile soils laden with moisture, my tendency is to throw all my energy (sugar) into growing shoots and leaves, because there seems no risk to my life, so I may as well flourish where I am—no need to send energy to the grapes, because I don't need the birds.

If I'm growing in a less fertile space and water is short, I'm thinking I need to get outta here because I might die. The best way to do that is not to grow leaves, but to put all my energy into the grapes and make them sweet and delicious for birds, then my seed is spread. Sweet and delicious for birds also means great for winemaking: simple as that. That's where the term 'a struggling vine makes the best wine' comes from.

But it's a fine line. Too much struggle means super-high sugar (or no sugar, because all my leaves fall off!), no acid, tough tannins, flabby flavours; too little struggle, too little sugar, high acids, thin wines.[2]

A certain level of healthy stress is necessary for ripening quality, complex fruit.

But when we think of stress, we tend to associate this negatively with the ways we are overwhelmed with the world's demands: the stress of heavy workloads, tight deadlines, and high expectations. This kind of stress is related to *the Productivity-Driven Approach* of overproduction—when we try to do too much.

As research suggests, this kind of stress produces health problems like high blood pressure, fatigue, anxiety, depression, burnout, and impaired performance. It's often referred to as "distress," because it has a negative effect. But, this is not the kind of stress our loving Vinedresser has intended for us. Remember, the goal of the vinedresser is not to pressure the vine into overproduction that will ultimately crash the vine. The goal is not quantity, the goal is *quality*.

---

2. Steve Smith, quoted in *"Smith & Sheth and Pyramid Valley Winemaking,"* *Decanter*, accessed October 30, 2024, https://www.decanter.com/learn/why-do-stressed-vines-produce-better-wines-ask-decanter-438655/.

There's a difference between the stress of overproduction and the healthy stress that comes from facing the real-world challenges needed to grow into who we're meant to be and bear the fruit we're meant to produce.

Frederick Douglass, a former slave and leading abolitionist, understood firsthand the stress of ripening quality fruit. In pursuing the fruit of equality in a society resistant to change, he wrote:

> If there's no struggle, there is no progress. Those who profess to favor freedom, and yet depreciate agitation, are men who want crops without plowing up the ground ... This struggle may be a moral one, or it may be a physical one, or it may be both moral and physical; but it must be a struggle.[3]

Here, he challenged those who claimed to support freedom, but were unwilling to face the discomfort and disruption that meaningful progress requires. Much like veraison, where the grape endures intense pressure to change color, accumulate sugars, and develop flavor, Douglass argued that justice and freedom demand a willingness to face hardships that transform both the individual and society.

A Different Kind of Stress

In psychological terms, this kind of healthy stress is called *eustress*. One definition of eustress is, "physical, mental, [spiritual] or emotional tension that is caused by something positive or is

---

3. Frederick Douglass, "West India Emancipation," speech, August 3, 1857, in *The Frederick Douglass Papers*, Series One: Speeches, Debates, and Interviews, vol. 3, ed. John W. Blassingame (New Haven, CT: Yale University Press, 1985), 204.

psychologically or physically beneficial."[4] The results of this kind of stress are that we have matured, grown a particular skill, and feel energized and engaged.

It's also important to note that this stress arises from focusing our attention into ripening one particular area for a short period of time. We were not made to live in a season of veraison forever.

My friend Bethany told me that when she was visiting Italy, she talked to local vinedressers about the stress of veraison. The translation she learned for the Italian word *stress* is more akin to the words, "to suffer" or "struggle."

Just as vines must struggle to ripen quality fruit, love matures to its fullest potential through meaningful suffering.

Christ, the True Vine, offers the ultimate example—enduring profound suffering on our behalf and ripening a love that lasts for eternity.

When stress arises in the pursuit of loving God with all our *heart, mind, soul, and strength*, and loving others as ourselves, it fosters growth, resilience, and the formation of sweet, lasting fruit. This process calls us to give ourselves wholly to God and others through the healthy exertion of these faculties, stretching us toward deeper love and maturity.

The Stress of the Heart

> It's the strain of sitting with another's pain, unsure of what to say or do, that matures our capacity for empathy.

4. *"Eustress,"* Dictionary.com, April 13, 2024, https://www.dictionary.com/e/word-of-the-day/eustress-2024-04-13/.

> ❧ It's the daily pressures of managing the chaos of children that slowly softens our impatience and cultivates self-control.

The Stress of the Mind

> ❧ It's the difficulty of learning a new language or skill that ripens our minds to be more adaptive.

> ❧ It's the uncertainty of starting a new business or ministry that strengthens our problem-solving skills.

The Stress of the Soul

> ❧ It's the challenge of taking risks in obedience to Jesus that grows our courage and deepens our dependence on God.

> ❧ It's the resistance and discomfort we face in the pursuit of justice that forges the resilience needed to create lasting change in our communities.

The Stress of Our Strength (Body)

> ❧ It's the physical demands of marathon training that gradually build the endurance needed to finish the race.

> ❧ It's the strain of serving in harsh weather or uncomfortable conditions that strengthens our resolve to serve faithfully.

Each of these forms of holy stress—heart, mind, soul, and strength—becomes a refining force that matures us to look more like Jesus. And often, the most formative lessons come not in grand gestures, but in the ordinary pressure points of daily life.

Softening in Stress

It was a frantic Friday morning in September. I had planned to meet Dave in the vineyard to talk about veraison after I dropped the kids off at the bus stop. As I corralled the kids to get ready for school, I was harried because we were running late. On my way to the bus stop, I pulled into my neighbor's driveway to turn my car around so I could park facing the bus stop.

The woman who owned the house was in her driveway and was visibly angry at me, waving her hands up in the air and giving me a glare as she walked back into the house. At that moment, in the stress of being late, I had a choice. Would I harden or soften toward this woman?

I took a deep breath and looked at my boys, "I think our neighbor is upset that I used her driveway. She looks pretty angry. Will you come with me to apologize?"

My youngest, Winston, was brave enough to come with me. We knocked on her door and apologized. Even after apologizing profusely, she was still very angry, and it was clear that this had been an issue for a long time—people using her driveway. She was mostly upset about it because during the winter months, it packed down the snow and made it difficult to shovel.

It was right after this conversation that I met Dave in the vine-yards, and he told me that as the vines undergo stress, they are softening. I don't know about you, but when I am stressed, I don't soften. I harden myself against any interruptions, people, or things that would get in the way of getting things done. But, what if we could undergo stress and ripen in a way that softens us—even sweetens us toward those around us?

On my drive home, I thought about my neighbor. I was tempted to harden against her. I mean, who gets so angry about people reversing in their driveway!? But, the Spirit gently nudged me and said, "Bette, she is your neighbor."

Suddenly, I remembered the Scripture passage the boys and I had read the night before: the Good Samaritan in Luke 10. Jesus asked the expert in the law, "who was the neighbor?" in the story.

The answer? The one who had shown mercy.

I felt my heart softening toward this woman, wondering what her life was like and whether or not her anger had to do with something more than just the driveway. The devotional we had read challenged us to do something kind for one of our neighbors.

I knew who I needed to be a neighbor to: the woman whom I had just angered. After talking it over with the boys, we decided to bake her some cookies as a peace offering and apology.

I confess that this isn't always how I respond in stress, but since talking with Dave, I have been wrestling with these questions, and I invite you to wrestle with me:

- How can I soften toward others when I am under stress, especially when they are the source of that stress?

- How can I soften toward myself when I am under the pressure of a deadline?

- How can I soften to the pain of the world, refusing to harden against it in apathy as my schedule fills up?

Could it be that the fruit sweetens in the softening?

We soften when we respond with empathy to the suffering of others. As we do, our hearts are tenderized, ripened, and readied for harvest. Conflict, discomfort, and stress, far from being obstacles, are the very processes that produce maturity, depth, and an enduring impact. The kind that at the end of the day might leave us tired, but deeply satisfied.

Good Stress or Bad Stress?

The question we must ask ourselves when under stress is this: Is this *eustress*, the healthy tension that comes with ripening, or *distress*, the strain of overproduction?

Is it the kind of stress that focuses our energy and attention on the work God is truly calling us to? The kind that invites restraint, asking us to pour ourselves only into what God has given us to ripen in this season? The kind that presses us to draw deeply from God's presence and provision?

Or is it the stress of spreading ourselves too thin, trying to ripen more than we were made to produce?

I can look back on seasons when I had so much going on that no one thing was able to fully ripen and mature. But I've also experienced times of intense pressure that felt purposeful, like an invitation to dig deep, persevere, and bring something beautiful to fruition.

As always with the vine, discernment is relational. As branches, we must continually ask: How are we partnering with the Vine (our identity), the Vinedresser (our cultivator), the Spirit (our life source), and the other branches (our community) to discern what leads to healthy veraison, and what will burn us out in the long run?

Veraison calls us to return again and again to Jesus, allowing the wisdom, gifts, and energy he has generously entrusted to us to ripen, through stress, into the fruit of his life, poured out in love for others.

Digging Deeper:

1. How have you experienced the difference between "good stress" and "bad stress" in your life? How has each shaped you?

2. In what ways might God be inviting you to soften and sweeten during stress? What could that look like in ordinary moments?

3. How can you partner with God to nurture and protect the fruit in your life (like a vine grower using bird netting) so it has the chance to fully mature?

Notes

Chapter 15:

Harvest

It is a brisk mid-October morning, and Happy Hour Lane is bustling with cars when I pull into Ten Hands Vineyard. The fog has just begun to lift, leaving a silver dew glistening along the grass. My tires crunch softly along the gravel road as I pass rows of Chardonnay vines, their leaves transformed from summer green to ochre yellow, dappled with dark maroon spots.

Ahead, a small group of harvesters in gardening gloves have gathered near a collection of empty, white, five-gallon buckets. A flutter of anticipation rises in me. The thrill of the harvest catches me by surprise, and I am eager to harvest grapes for the very first time.

It's also the first time I meet Tom Petzold, who stands between a row of vines commanding the group like a ship captain in a ball cap, hoodie, and rugged work vest. He gestures for everyone to follow him over to one of the vines as he explains the harvesting process.

As I take up my place in the circle around Tom, I feel a quiet reverence settle over me. I feel like I am intruding on something sacred, and I wonder whether I should be here. But as I glance around, I notice the others shifting their weight back and forth like sheepish children on the playground. It occurs to me that perhaps I am not the only novice here. I have found myself among a small collective of harvest newbies eagerly listening and nodding attentively to Tom in their winter hats.

After distributing pairs of picking shears, Tom demonstrates how to clip each cluster off the vine with care. He lifts a bunch to his nose, showing us how to detect the scent of vinegar, and how to recognize grapes that must be discarded.

Once he dismisses us, I stand in front of a vine flush with grapes glowing like lanterns in the morning sun. The clusters are the size of a handful of large marbles, and you can see the seeds beneath their translucent, leathery, yellow skin. They are speckled with dark brown spots that Tom calls "sunburn."

I catch sight of Dave as he walks up and down the vineyard, observing the harvesting process. He is cracking a few jokes to the old-timers, tossing a few grapes at people, and giving tips to novice harvesters as he does. "Everything we have talked about during the cultivation of the vine," he says, "leads up to this culminating moment right here—the harvest."

As I look down the rows of vines, I see a whole community of family members and friends sitting on overturned buckets in front of the vines like farmers milking cows. They delicately but rapidly clip clusters of grapes and drop them into a second bucket nearby. It is all done by hand.

Tom weaves through the vineyard in a squeaky golf cart, swapping full buckets for empty ones and dumping the grapes into half-ton plastic bins. These will be hauled to the winery and processed the very same day.

As I settle into the rhythm of clipping the grapes off the vine one by one, I am flooded with joy. And with it, a holy weight of what harvest means in the kingdom of God.

A Sense of Urgency

There's a reason the harvest carries a sacred urgency. Grapes must be gathered at just the right moment. If farmers don't act quickly, the harvest will be lost. For a few brief weeks, everything hinges on this. The time is now, and all hands are on deck to gather it in.

Jesus knew this urgency.

The three years of his ministry were like an imperative harvest time. There was always a need for workers to partner with him in the work of healing, deliverance, and teaching. In Matthew 9, he looks at the crowd with compassion and says to his disciples: "The harvest is plentiful but the workers are few. Ask the Lord of the harvest, therefore, to send out workers into his harvest field."[1]

When harvest comes, it is a *kairos* moment. In one of her sermons, Danielle Strickland named *kairos* moments as "an invasion of eternity into the present tense; a sacred and holy interruption to our everyday life [with an] invitation to partner with God in the coming kingdom."

---

1. Matthew 9:37-38.

The implication in a *kairos* moment is that the conditions are ripe for action. It's a call to be fully present and respond to God's invitation to partner in his in-breaking kingdom, harvesting what he has been quietly ripening within us and in the world.

My friend Bethany explained what this journey has looked like for her. Over the last year, she sensed God's invitation to invest five of her 25 ministry hours each week to simply abiding in Jesus, cultivating intimacy through the Ignatian spiritual practices. On the surface, it didn't appear to produce anything tangible. It was a lot of slow internal work to cultivate loving attachment to Jesus.

Then, several months later, came a moment that called for a harvest. Her pastor's teenage son died suddenly on a Monday. By midweek, the elders had asked Bethany to deliver the sermon that coming Sunday. "All of a sudden," she told me, "it felt like God began to draw out what he had already been ripening in me. The sermon just sort of wrote itself because it was what God had been cultivating in me for a long time. And now it was just the right time to give this message to my community grieving this tragic and unexpected loss."

She described how those hidden, seemingly unproductive hours alone with Jesus had been preparing her in ways she couldn't yet see. God had not only been ripening the message, but also her heart. Her character had been quietly shaped in her time with Jesus, enabling her to speak with a spirit of humility, empathy, and compassion.

There are moments when we are called to bring forth a harvest of love through our words, presence, or sacrificial action. This kind of fruit grows from a life rooted deep in our connection to the Vine.

As we explored earlier, when we've allowed the Vinedresser to cultivate us through many seasons of Christ's death, resurrection, and life, we find ourselves ready when the time is ripe for harvest. And when that moment comes, we won't want to keep it to ourselves. Because harvest is not something that can be experienced in isolation. Harvest, by its nature, is a communal experience.

A Communal Experience

During my third harvest at Ten Hands, I walked up and down the rows with Dave, meeting various friends and family members of his and Tom Petzold's. Some had come up from Texas to experience their first harvest, while local veterans had been harvesting these vines for decades.

"Harvest time is incredibly inclusive," Dave later told me. "You have a smattering of all kinds of people doing this together. Whoever wants to pick is welcome." Among the harvesters were also several vineyard owners from the surrounding area who had come to lend a hand. Unlike many industries defined by competition, there was familiarity, generosity, and shared joy. They knew each other's names and welcomed one another's help.

As the older, more experienced vineyard owners harvested side by side, they shared tips: how they managed mildew that season, when they chose to prune, and how they cared for the soil. Occasionally, they also offered guidance to the novices, like me, who were pretending to know what we were doing.

When I asked several of them how they felt about the harvest, the answer was unanimous: "This is the best part. This is what we've been working toward all year." There was a sense of camaraderie between them. And you just knew—they took care of one another. Undoubtedly, when it came harvest time on their vineyards, Tom would be out there with his baseball cap and work vest, clipping away.

Even when we're gathering the fruits of a journey that feels largely solitary, it's worth recognizing how significant a role community has been to our formation along the way. Often, the same people who walked with us through long, hidden seasons of dormancy are the ones who show up to celebrate the harvest. We cannot grow or gather the fruits of God's work within us alone.

Scripture reflects this too: harvest was a communal celebration marked by joy. Israel's calendar revolved around harvest time, with major festivals themed around it: Passover, the Feast of Pentecost, and the Feast of Booths.[2] Psalm 126 speaks of those who "sow in tears" reaping "with songs of joy," in communal celebration. The reality is, we need one another to both gather the harvest and celebrate the fruits of our labor.

The Abundant Harvest

Five years after the *Beauty and the Formation of the Soul* retreat, I found myself driving back down to the Hermitage Retreat Center. Buckled into the back seat like a child were the eighteen original paintings from my first book, *Making Room in Advent*. Throughout the drive, I was overflowing with joy—eager to return these pieces to the place that had shaped them and to share them with the retreat community in the months ahead, including the upcoming Advent retreat in December.

As I worked with the directors, Troy and Faith, to install the paintings in their Phoenix gallery, I placed the book on a shelf beside the artwork and paused to take it all in. These paintings—and the book itself—were the harvest of countless seeds sown in me at the Hermitage over the years. Standing there, I felt the deep fulfillment of a sacred cycle: witnessing the fruit of seeds planted

---

2. Ryken, Wilhoit, and Longman, *Dictionary of Biblical Imagery*, 365.

long ago, now brought to harvest after many years of abiding in the Vine.

I stayed an extra day for a personal silent retreat. As I walked toward the spiral labyrinth, the landscape was bursting with life. A sprawling sumac bush near the entrance had nearly doubled in size since my last visit, stretching thirty feet long and ten feet high. Its clusters of deep red seed cones flared like flames against the green canopy. When I stepped into the labyrinth, I could hardly see the spiral, it was so overgrown. The boundaries of the path were brimming with goldenrods as tall as me. I was surprised by how much the wildlife had grown over the last five years. Then the Lord reminded me, "As have you."

When I first came to the Hermitage in 2019, I was entering a season of dormancy—a time when the seeds God planted in me needed to rest and take root, hidden in the dark. Now, five years later, I had stepped into a season of harvest, and the signs were all around me. Wanting to lean into the metaphor, I offered to help Troy and Faith gather vegetables from the community garden they had planted that spring. They enthusiastically received my help and walked me through the garden—pointing out what was ripe for picking and what still needed time.

The "Sabbath Garden," as it's called, is divided into seven sections: one plot rests each year, another is planted with cover crops to nourish the soil, and the others brim with fruits and vegetables. The resting plot rotates counterclockwise each year, echoing the rhythm we've explored throughout this book—life, death, and resurrection.

As I picked, I felt like a child playing hide and seek with the vegetables hidden beneath the canopies of leaves. With each bulb of yellow squash or green zucchini, I whispered, "found you." It wasn't long before I waddled back to the Hermitage kitchen with two grocery bags and a wicker basket overflowing with vegetables.

When I slumped my haul down onto the kitchen counter, Faith laughed and asked, "Well, would you like to take any produce home?"

I protested, "But don't you need these vegetables for the people coming here on retreat?"

She smiled, "Bette, I have six bags of frozen shredded zucchini in the fridge and several buckets of tomatoes still waiting to be canned. The harvest is abundant, and abundance is meant to be shared."

> *The harvest is abundant, and abundance is meant to be shared.*

I turned that phrase over and over in my mind that day and have been chewing on it ever since.

The Harvest Is Meant to Be Shared

As those entrusted with God's harvest field and bearers of Jesus' presence in the world, we carry the sacred opportunity to share the fruit of that harvest with others. We are invited to steward God's abundance in ways that cultivate the shalom of all creation—through generosity, interdependence, and justice.

In God's design, we are not isolated individuals, but deeply connected to one another and the rest of creation. When one part suffers, it affects the whole. If we are truly God's family, then we feel one another's losses in the same way we would one of our own relatives. Recognizing this interconnectedness and responding by sharing God's abundance is the essence of living justly.

Justice, in this sense, is not abstract. It is tangible, embodied in how we care for one another. All of creation—plants, animals, humans, and the land—is interwoven. Justice comes alive when we act on this truth, creating a world where all have equal access to the resources needed to thrive. In doing so, we reflect the generosity and interdependence embedded in creation itself.

In Scripture, God's heart for justice is revealed in the commands given to the Israelites in the Old Testament. The Mosaic law in Leviticus and Deuteronomy instructs farmers to share their abundance with the poor and the foreigner by leaving the edges of their fields unharvested and not gathering what was left behind.[3]

The Dictionary of Biblical Imagery notes: "Harvest was accompanied by feelings of generosity awakened by the sight of the poor of a community being provided for as they gleaned in the fields owned by others."[4]

This practice was more than an act of charity, it was an act of God's justice. It was a reflection of his heart: the heart of a God who cares deeply for the well-being of the most vulnerable.

When the Israelites failed to uphold this call, God had some strong words. Isaiah declares:

"It is you who have ruined my vineyard; the plunder from the poor is in your houses."[5]

Gisela Kreglinger expands on this in *The Spirituality of Wine*:

> When the poor, vulnerable, and marginalized are forgotten—or worse, oppressed—this treatment will affect the health of the whole vineyard. God's vineyard will only flourish when

---

3. Leviticus 19:9–10 and 23:22; Deuteronomy 24:19–22.

4. Ryken, Wilhoit, and Longman, *Dictionary of Biblical Imagery*, 365.

5. Isaiah 3:14.

the stronger and more powerful will reach out to the weaker and more vulnerable, and when they learn together what it means to flourish in God's vineyard. A biblical understanding of human flourishing is very different from a contemporary emphasis on maximizing productivity and profit. Living souls cannot be reduced to economic actors, nor can they flourish spiritually as isolated individuals.[6]

As we explored in Chapter 2, the *way* we harvest matters just as much as *what* we harvest. And the way of God's harvest is always love. As we abide in Jesus, the True Vine, we are formed by his love—a love that consistently centers the "othered" in society: the poor, the outcast, and the broken. To abide in Christ's love is to live as he did: bringing those left out of the story into the very center of it. This includes those who, from *the Productivity-Driven Approach*, are seen as lacking value or worth because of their inability to produce.

When we harvest only for personal gain—whether profit, power, or prestige—we risk perpetuating systems that exploit the very ones Christ came to lift up. This is the invitation of the harvest: to let the overflowing fruit of God's work within us become sustenance that nourishes others. Because abundance is meant to be shared.

A Harvest That Multiplies

After harvesting vegetables at the Sabbath Garden, Faith prepared a lavish meal from the garden's bounty: zucchini frittata, bruschetta with cucumbers and tomatoes, an Italian salad, roasted radishes, and pumpkin pie. The vibrant greens, reds, and oranges on my plate were a beauty unto themselves, embodying the extravagant generosity of God.

---

6. Kreglinger, *The Spirituality of Wine*, 201.

But the taste! If God's love could be made edible, this is what it would taste like: juicy tomatoes bursting with flavor, the bright zip of vinegar, and the crunch of cucumbers layered together on crusty bread. The bruschetta paired perfectly with the savory frittata made from eggs gathered that morning from the chickens I'd seen scuttling through the yard.

Like a vinedresser crafting grapes into wine, Faith's hands transformed humble ingredients into a feast that nourished both body and soul. With each bite, joy welled up. When I set my fork down, full and satisfied, I whispered my thanks to the Lord of the Harvest.

The nourishment I received carried me home with renewed love for my family and neighbors. And with plenty of vegetables still in hand, I was able to prepare meals that extended that same love outward. That's how the harvest works—it multiplies. It nourishes. It carries the flavor of the kingdom, spreading in a sacred cycle of generosity and reciprocity.

Digging Deeper:

1. Have you ever experienced a moment in your life that felt like a "*kairos* moment," a sacred and urgent invitation to harvest? How did you respond?

2. How have you experienced both the labor and joy of the harvest in your community?

3. Where is God inviting you to share the abundance of his harvest with others?

Chapter 16:

Wine

An hour after I get home from harvesting at Ten Hands Vineyard, I receive a text from Dave—they're transporting the grapes to Left Foot Charley's Winery for pressing. I jump out of my chair and rush over, arriving just as several large vats of grapes move from a forklift through the garage into the winery.

I feel like a VIP witnessing the behind-the-scenes magic that happens once a year. The energy in the room buzzes with excitement. The mechanical press hums loudly, blending with electrifying rock music, as a team of workers gather around the conveyor belt. Dave, standing among them, greets me with a smile and nods toward the ladder leading up to the top of the winepress. He hollers over the machines, "Go take a look!"

I race toward the ladder with wild enthusiasm, then slow my pace as I carefully climb the narrow rungs.

At the top, I peer through a small rectangular viewing hole and catch a glimpse of the grapes tumbling down the conveyor belt into the press. They cascade like rain in large green clumps. Below, the team of workers watch the grapes with laser focus, hands moving in quick bursts as they inspect each cluster before placing it back on the belt to continue its journey into the massive steel winepress.

The terracotta floor tiles glisten, wet with sticky grape juice. When I climb back down, I look into another rectangular opening at the bottom of the press, watching the juice flow freely through a pipe like a waterfall, collecting in a large steel drum.

Dave dips a wine glass into the fresh Chardonnay juice, lifts it to his nose, and inhales deeply. "Smells like lemon oil... a little grassy," he says.

He leads me on a tour through the winery, weaving through towering stainless-steel tanks that stretch nearly to the ceiling and the shorter, honey-pot-shaped, plastic vats. Each vessel holds juice from various local harvests, all at different stages of fermentation.

At each stop, Dave pours me a small taste. The juice is intensely sweet, vibrant, and delicious in its own right. But as I watch Dave sample each, I sense he envisions something more. The vinedresser has become the winemaker who longs to trans-form this raw sweetness into something complex and enduring. Something otherworldly.

As we walk from vat to vat, he explains the process.

"Just like in the growing season, a winemaker can make a thousand different decisions in how the wine is handled," he says. "Because I'm not making large batches for supermarkets, I can create unique variations from what I've been given each season. For the Chardonnay, I pressed the whole cluster. But for the Pinot Gris, I removed the stems and let them sit overnight before crushing. It all depends on what the fruit needs and the vision of what I'm after."

Because Dave chooses quality over quantity, he is able to tailor each small batch to express the unique story of that year's vintage and terroir.

Isn't this what God does with us?

As we surrender the harvest of our lives poured out in love, God receives these raw materials and crafts them into something beautiful, enduring, and distinct.

> Not mass-produced.
> Not rushed.
> But lovingly tended.
> Intentionally made.

The Master Vintner artfully shapes a wine that reflects the terroir of our stories, our circumstances, and our context—a wine that deepens in character and richness over time.

Just as the vine enters dormancy after harvest, so does the wine. As the wine rests, the sediment settles and the fermentation process completes. Rush this step, and the wine becomes unstable—clouded with residue and explosive pressure that can blow the corks out and ruin the batch.

And yet, how often do we try to rush the process of making new wine with Jesus?

We long to see the fruit of our labor, don't we? To witness the kingdom impact of our efforts. But the truth is, God never promised us immediate results.

Because the harvest doesn't belong to us.

It belongs to the Lord of the Harvest—the True Vinedresser and Winemaker—who alone sees the future. He will do with our offerings what he pleases, in his time.

> **Some years, we may not see fruit at all.**
>
> **Sometimes what we offer to the winepress won't be recognized or appreciated until long after we're gone.**
>
> **But that's not our responsibility.**
>
> **Our part is simply to yield.**

To become lasting, beautiful wine, grapes must surrender to pressing, fermentation, and the work of time. Only then can their true potential be revealed.

At the end of every harvest, we return once more to the cycle of death, resurrection, and life. We are invited to enter the winepress of Christ—where, in surrender, life begins anew.

Into the Winepress

In the harvest of his life, Jesus yielded beautiful fruit: lives were healed, sins were forgiven, and those who had been excluded were welcomed to the table. These fruits offered a foretaste of the kingdom of God, yet his mission was not complete.

For the new wine of God's covenant to emerge, Jesus surrendered to the winepress of suffering. In the garden, he sweats drops of blood under the crushing weight of loving obedience.

On the cross, when the soldier pierced his side, new wine flowed. In a holy mystery, the Spirit ferments this offering into the communion cup of the new covenant. When we drink from it, we partake of Christ himself: his forgiveness, his life, his love.

Just as grapes are transformed into enduring wine, we are united with Christ—and with one another—through his death in a bond that transcends time and space.

Together, through the pressing, we become the new wine poured out for the world.

As Paul writes, "Now if we are children, then we are heirs—heirs of God and co-heirs with Christ, if indeed we share in his sufferings in order that we may also share in his glory."[1]

Paul reminds us that when we are pressed—especially when suffering for our obedience to Jesus—we participate in the winepress of the cross. And in that pressing, his glory is revealed.

Making New Wine

Four years after my sabbatical, I sat in front of my computer screen, leading one of our monthly Infinitum online prayer days with people from all over the world. As I stared at the grid of faces, I felt like I had little left to offer, trying to drum up the energy and confidence to lead this group on the topic of lament.

---

1. Romans 8:17.

In every sense of the word, I felt wrung out. Like grapes crushed at the bottom of the winepress, the intense season of ministry had pressed down upon me with such force that whatever juice stored up in the crevices of my soul were quickly being squeezed out. Sometimes, what emerged was beautiful and looked like the kingdom. But if I'm honest, much of it was flat out rotten.

During a break in the session, when we each went offline to pray alone, I found myself circling around aimlessly in my art studio. That's when I saw it; a painting I had started in 2020 during the pandemic, one I'd titled *New Wine*. I had set it aside for years, unsure of where it was headed. But now, it called to me.

I put in my headphones and played the song "New Wine" by Hillsong United. As the lyrics poured out, "in the crushing, in the pressing, you are making new wine,"[2] I crushed the Alizarin Crimson, Indian Red, and Dioxazine Purple oil paints with my palette knife in rhythm with the music.

Slowly, I spread the paint in long strokes over the gold leaf and acrylic underpainting. The crimson grabbed the uneven gold leaf ridges in a visceral texture. And as I gently smoothed the brush through the paint, I released a wordless lament through each stroke. With only a few minutes before our next session started, I didn't have time to finish cleaning my brushes, so I set them aside and returned to the Zoom call.

In a breakout room, joined by participants from Germany, Canada, and the UK, I shared the unexplainable grief I was carrying from several difficult situations at our church. The same dynamic seemed to repeat itself, as if I were caught in a loop I couldn't escape. Each time, it reopened old wounds of rejection and marginalization. I found myself asking, "Why does this keep happening? Didn't I learn what God was trying to teach me?"

---

2. Hillsong United, *New Wine, There Is More* (Hillsong Music Australia, 2018).

Despite my desire to grow, my response hadn't changed much. I was still knotted up in anger and bitterness.

As we prayed and listened, my friend Ian from the UK described an image that came to him in prayer. He said tenderly in his beautiful British accent:

> I could picture you, Bette, on this continual cycle of grief. I saw you physically making that journey, I guess. But as you fell and stumbled, you reached out to steady yourself on the ground. As you got up and looked at your hands, they were covered with a color. An unfamiliar color—one that was quite possibly new in tone, depth, and richness. It was as if on each cycle, your hands found new color, contrast, and mixtures. These colors were not just for you, but for the world, and as you paint and incorporate those colors, tones and mixtures into your work, we will benefit and discover a deeper understanding of who we are.

Fermentation

As Ian shared his vision, I remembered something Dave once showed me—how grapes change color during fermentation. As the sugars break down and transform into alcohol, a new hue emerges. Skin-fermented Pinot Gris, for example, when left in contact with the skins, takes on an unexpected and beautiful amber or orange tone.

As we finished praying, I stared down at my hands, palms up resting on my laptop. They were stained with oil paint the color of wine. I had not, in fact, used that particular mixture of pigments before. The tones were unfamiliar. It was as though, through the pressing, God was creating something new—something not just for me, but for the world.

As we commune with Christ in the winepress, we participate in ongoing spiritual fermentation. Just as the grape juice is converted into a more enduring substance, the essence of our old selves—the sinful patterns destined to waste away—is taken up by Christ and converted into a new self that is deeper and more enduring.

For some, this might look like the person once quick to take offense and anger that gradually transmutes into someone more resilient, patient, and forgiving over time.

For others, it's the crushing and overwhelming process of grief that creates an expanded capacity to comfort others.

Some choose to live among the poor, not out of obligation, but out of love for those on the margins. Over time, their lives become rich with compassion, offering a taste of the kingdom on earth.

And then there are those who have lived their entire lives in poverty, yet somehow ferment a joy, gratitude, and love that offers a pure taste of heaven. These lives are often the most stunning examples of beautiful wine often overlooked, but deeply potent and wholly sacred.

And still, sometimes, the crushing doesn't feel holy. Sometimes it just feels excruciatingly painful. Yet even there, the invitation remains: to surrender again and again to the winemaker's hands—to the One who tenderly crafts something beautiful, even out of the pain of pressing. He will not let it destroy us, but in his mercy, he will create something new.

As Paul writes, we may be "hard pressed on every side, but not crushed."[3] Like grapes in the winepress, "we always carry around

---

3. 2 Corinthians 4:8.

in our body the death of Jesus, so that the life of Jesus may also be revealed in our body."[4]

When we love sacrificially, when we are pressed by life and yet still choose to follow Jesus, we release the flavor and fragrance of Christ into the atmosphere.

The pressing, the crushing, the long work of fermentation, these are not just trials to endure. They are the sacred processes that shape the very flavor of our lives into an offering of love poured out to a world that desperately needs it.

New Wineskins

The shape of the vessel where the wine ferments and ages profoundly influences its taste. Dave once told me that the same fruit, placed in different vessels, will be noticeably different the next day. But, discerning the right "container" for new wine isn't just a technical decision, it's a spiritual one.

In Jesus' time, wine wasn't stored in the large vats we see today. It was poured into wineskins—flexible pouches made from animal hides. These skins were ideal for fermentation because they could stretch as the wine expanded. But as Jesus warned, people do not "pour new wine into old wineskins. If they do, the skins will burst; the wine will run out and the wineskins will be ruined. No, they pour new wine into new wineskins, and both are preserved."[5]

This metaphor reveals something profound: when God is doing something new, it cannot be contained in old structures, mindsets, or ways of doing things. The old wineskins, having already

---

4. 2 Corinthians 4:10.

5. Matthew 9:17.

been stretched and worn, aren't able to hold the expansive work that new wine requires. If we insist on trying to preserve the old, the very thing we're trying to protect—the new wine God is creating—will be lost in the process.

When God is making new wine in our lives, it often means we have to let go of the old containers: the systems and structures we have relied on to hold the wine for so long. These can no longer contain the fresh work he's doing.

This is not a call to discard everything from the past, but to recognize when something new is being birthed and to be open to the change required to embrace it. The new wine requires vessels that are supple, open, and willing to stretch.

In one conversation with my spiritual director, I shared how crushed I felt in that season when God was making new wine in my life. She gently replied, "Yes, and you've been trying to pour it into old wineskins. No wonder they're bursting."

She was right. In my desire to offer what God was forming within me, I kept trying to pour it into old structures—places that had once held me well, but could no longer contain the new thing God was doing. Again and again, the result was the same: the wineskin burst.

In one moment of prayer, I found myself lamenting as I imagined all this beautiful, valuable wine that Jesus and I had created together spilling all over the floor and dripping through the cracks.

But immediately, I felt Jesus interrupt this thought:

"Bette, don't think I will waste a single drop. Yes, the new wine is being poured out and it is spilling all over the floor. But can you see this instead like the alabaster jar of perfume broken and poured out on my feet?"

Jesus reminded me of the woman in Mark 14 who broke her alabaster jar and anointed him with expensive perfume. As her extremely generous act of worship spilled all over the floor, her accusers called it a waste.

But Jesus defended her: "She has done a beautiful thing to me."[6]

I needed to receive these words for myself.

Even as the accuser's voice whispered, "What a waste," Jesus called it beautiful.

Later, I shared that image with a few trusted friends. As they prayed for me, one of them saw something more: the new wine I had poured out didn't just spill onto the floor. It started dripping through the cracks in the floorboard. In the room below, there was a group of people thirsty, yearning, and aching for new wine. As the wine slipped through the cracks, they kept their mouths open to receive it with joy and gratitude.

Listen. I don't know what kind of new wine Jesus is making through you.

I don't know how you have been pressed to become who you are, or how you have wept when the wineskin you thought could hold you burst, but let me tell you something:

Jesus will not waste a single drop.

Whatever we pour out in worship upon Jesus is never a waste.
The world may not recognize the preciousness of what you offer, but Jesus does.
Others may call it a waste, but Jesus calls it beautiful.
And just like that alabaster jar, what we pour out for him becomes a fragrance that lingers for generations.

---

6. Mark 14:6.

He receives it, honors it, and multiplies its impact.
We can still smell the perfume in that story, can't we?

In the same way, Jesus transforms the harvest of love we offer into wine that endures, growing richer, more complex, and more beautiful with pressing and time.

A Taste of the Kingdom of God

One summer, I visited Bos Wine Garden in Elk Rapids with a few friends. Dave and his wife, Jackie, had recently opened the space—a dream they had carried together for years. As I mentioned in the introduction, this garden was the fruit of their shared vision. Dave cultivates the vines; Jackie cultivates the table and the atmosphere where they are enjoyed. He is the gardener; she is the host.

Behind the quaint farmhouse-turned-winery, we stepped into a stunning patio surrounded by lush flowers and cover crops. Jackie's intentional touches were everywhere. From the colors and textures to the embossed plates and thoughtfully set tables.

Dave's vinedressing philosophy of quality over quantity was mirrored in the way Jackie designed the space. Their love for vines, for the wine, for one another, and for their guests over-flowed into every square inch of that little patio.

We were greeted by Dave's sister, Elizabeth, who guided us through a pairing menu, each wine thoughtfully matched with bites that would draw out its richness and nuance.

Something about sitting there—savoring little bites of cheese and prosciutto paired with the wine, surrounded by gardens inten-tionally cultivated with cover crops used in the vineyard—felt entirely sacramental.

Everything was so *intentional*. So layered with meaning and depth. Each element building upon one another and weaving together to create a rich feast for all the senses. The beauty and mystery of what we experienced that afternoon is hard to describe.

At one point, Dave sauntered over to the table and reached for a yellow mustard plant nearby, used for cover cropping. He pulled it from the ground and, to Jackie's horror, laid it on the patio table. Holding the root structure delicately between his fingers, he pointed out the nodules that push essential natural nitrogen into the soil that fuels the vines.

That moment took me back to when I first met Dave. I had an endless stream of questions:

How does a vine produce fruit?
What does it mean to abide in the vine?
How does a vinedresser cultivate vines?

But I realized that day that the answers were not just in Dave's words. They were in the wine itself. Each glass held a culmination of creativity, inspiration, and years of tending—not just to the vines, but to the soil, the story, and most of all, the people.

What made the experience complete—what brought their dream to life—was not just the wine, or the food, or even the beauty of the setting. It was the relationships: the guests, friends, and family gathered together around the table to savor it all together.

As we looked around, taking in the sight of that little community scattered around the wine garden, it felt utterly sacred. My friends and I just kept stealing glances with one another, whispering, "This is so beautiful ... so rich." It was almost too much to take in.

In the wine garden, we caught a glimpse of what loving union overflowing with beauty, blessing, and abundance looks like. The garden embodied the dream Dave and Jackie had carried together: a marriage poured out for the sake of others at the table.

Some moments become windows into another world—a glimpse of heaven here and now, among these people, in this place. That afternoon felt like a glimmer of the kingdom of God.

Because the story that began in a vineyard culminates at the table—at a feast overflowing from another kind of marriage union—the union of heaven and earth, Christ and his beloved, at the wedding feast of the Lamb.

The Wedding Feast of the Lamb

As Isaiah prophesied:

> On this mountain the Lord Almighty will prepare
>   a feast of rich food for all peoples,
> a banquet of aged wine—
>   the best of meats and the finest of wines.
> On this mountain he will destroy
>   the shroud that enfolds all peoples,
> the sheet that covers all nations;
>   he will swallow up death forever.
> The Sovereign Lord will wipe away the tears
>   from all faces;
> he will remove his people's disgrace
>   from all the earth.
> The Lord has spoken.[7]

At the end of all things, we will gather at that banquet. Jesus, the Bridegroom, will take our hand—his beloved Bride—and gently

---

7. Isaiah 25:6-8.

wipe every tear from our eyes. With the delight and pride of a groom on his wedding day, he will lead us to the feast.

There, we will celebrate our union:
wrapped in joy, abundance, and beauty
beyond imagination.
That eternal table will be set with the finest wine,
echoing all the little communion feasts that came before it,
yet far surpassing them in glory.

God the Vinedresser becomes the host.
He sets the table with the richest of foods,
inviting all peoples to share in its abundance.

No longer will the cheap wine run out.
No longer will our cups be empty—
poured out by all our striving
to earn belovedness, belonging, and blessing.

Like the wedding at Cana,
he will remove our disgrace,
And transform our scarcity into sumptuousness.

On that day, the finest wine will spill over without end—
the fruit of a covenant fully realized,
a joy made complete,
a love made whole.
a world made new.

The wine poured out
will be the overflow of a loving union
cultivated over many vintages and terroirs;
shaped by the tender hand of the Vinedresser;
ripened through our abiding in the True Vine
And our connection to one another.
Pressed and fermented,

it will be shared in sacred celebration
at the restoration of all things.

And when we receive a glass of this wine,
our senses—especially our sense of smell,
so intimately tied to memory—will awaken.

In its aroma, we'll remember
the love of the Lamb who was slain,
poured out for us.

And as we lift the cup to our lips,
we will taste the loving intimacy of his presence—
the True Vine who remained in us
through every stage of the journey,
and the Vinedresser who formed us
into who we were always meant to be.

Digging Deeper:

1. Is there any area of your life where you are experiencing
    being "pressed?" How is God transforming you and your fruit
    through this?

2. How might God be inviting you or your faith community to
    let go of "old wineskins" to make room for the new wine he is
    creating at this time?

3. What has God been forming in you on the journey from vine
    to table? Who needs to be invited to the feast?

Epilogue

It is mid-February when I return to the Hermitage to pick up the Advent paintings, months after the retreat. It seems fitting that I would finish this book here—the terroir that shaped so much of this story.

When I pull into the drive, I pass the familiar sign that says, "begin to slow down" and smile. The ground is covered in snow, and as I near the parking lot, I catch a glimpse of the Sabbath garden. Once full of wild energy in October, with hidden treasures of zucchini and butternut squash beneath its leaves, it has quieted down for a rest, for a Sabbath, like its name. Even the tall 10-foot stalks of corn have been taken out to prepare for the garden's reconfiguration in spring.

Troy, Faith, and I take the paintings down from the gallery, making room for a new exhibit they will hang for Lent. And somehow, it feels right. It's time for something new. After buckling the paintings into the back of my car, I take a short walk to the labyrinth. The only sound is the crunch of snow beneath my feet as I near the large sumac bush, tall enough to walk beneath. Its bare branches are now home to at least fifty robins. They hop back and forth between branches, nervous at my approach.

As I step beneath the canopy, they suddenly take off in a flurry of red and brown, disappearing toward the horizon. I've learned that robins symbolize the end of winter and the start of a new growth cycle—a new chapter. In the Christian tradition, they also represent the death and resurrection of Christ. Their presence reminds me that this is a threshold moment. As I finish this book and prepare for the start of Lent, I sense the liminal space between the completion of harvest and the descent into dormancy, where God will awaken something new.

The medieval labyrinth is covered in snow, but I can still make out a path between the foot-high collection of twigs and brush, remnants of October's overgrowth. We are past the winter solstice now, and the days are slowly growing longer. Beneath the snow, life stirs in quiet anticipation, waiting to unfold in due time. As I follow the winding path, curving back and forth as it gradually leads to the center, I gather items to create a small altar and reflect on where this journey began—right here at the Hermitage.

I think of the driven, achievement-oriented leader who arrived here six years ago for the *Beauty and the Formation of the Soul* retreat. I see her striving so hard to prove herself—to earn approval—and I want to whisper to her, "You don't have to earn your belovedness. You already have it."

I remember the tenderness with which I walked the spiral laby-rinth, feeling held in the womb of God on the verge of new creation. And then, I recall the moments of profound healing at the retreat, when Jesus came for the wounded and captive artist, setting her free from the walls of shame that had kept her from creating. And I smile, thinking of the eighteen paintings buckled in my back seat—the fruits of that liberation.

Looking back, I see that I'm still driven, but softened, perhaps, by creation's rhythms, and more mindful of the influence of *the Productivity-Driven Approach* on me. I am less concerned with quick and tangible results, and more willing to take the long journey—to abide in Christ through the slow, cyclical spiral of his life, death, and resurrection. The more I have practiced abiding in Jesus through every season, the more I have become one with the Vine. His life has become my life. His death, my death. His resurrection, my resurrection.

In every dormant season, he has been leading me deeper into the roots of his love, reminding me of my belovedness as I abide with him. As I surrender the temptation to measure success by external metrics, I die to the impulse of my false self and awaken to the true self that emerges from the roots of the inner life.

It is there, out of the depths of silence, solitude, and stillness, where I emerge in bud break with new dreams. These dreams don't come from striving, but from being so loved by Jesus that it oozes up like sap from the roots. They overflow into the community of branches with the explosive power of resurrection.

As this vibrant energy breaks through internal and external resistance in my life, I am learning how to trust its flow; the Holy Spirit's creative spark that is abundantly generous. The more I vulnerably open myself, like a flower among the branches of community, the more I experience what it means to be seen, soothed, safe, and secure. In that space, I can emerge into my truest self. And when I extend this gift to others, I enter the beautiful dance of reciprocity that sets the fruit of the kingdom.

As I reach the center of the labyrinth, I stop and close my eyes, breathing in the fresh, cold air. Without the buzz of bees, the swaying goldenrod, and the rustling leaves, the valley is largely still, save for the distant chirping of robins, the faint caw of a crow, and the rhythmic peck of a woodpecker on a dormant tree.

In my arms, I carry a collection of dry twigs, reed grass, wildflowers, and sumac fruit clusters—emblems of the stories, people, and gifts gathered along this journey. I lay them down in the snow, one by one, and create a little altar of gratitude for all God has done over the last five years, and for the person I've become along the way.

As I gaze at the beautiful collection of dried offerings resting in the snow, I think about this book you now hold in your hands, a tangible expression of the fruit cultivated in my life over these years. This fruit has been pressed and poured out for you, fermenting within the editing process into the pages themselves.

And I hope, like all good wine, it lingers on your lips and awakens another world within you—an ecstasy of God's love that, when received, becomes part of you.

As you've journeyed through this book, I hope you've uncovered your own story of abiding, one that, in time, bears a fruit of lasting quality, drawn from the shared branches among us. The kind of fruit that ripens slowly through careful cultivation in every season, and overflows from our connection to the Vine. So that, little by little, we might become ever more radiant with the fruits of the Spirit, ripening:

> Even more love.
> Even more joy.
> Even more peace.
> Even more patience.
> Even more kindness.
> Even more goodness.
> Even more faithfulness.
> Even more gentleness.
> And yes—even more self-control.

This is the kind of fruit the world desperately needs right now, even if they don't know it yet. The cheap wine has run out, friends. So, in a world that is depleted, worn out, and aching for beauty, my prayer for you, dear reader, is this:

A Benediction

> May you resist the impulse to generate fruit
> by your own strength, control, or performance,
> producing cheap wine that leaves
> those around you thirsty.
>
> Instead, may you find liberation
> from the demands of efficiency, quantity, and success,

relaxing into the cultivation of a Vinedresser
who loves you and desires your flourishing.

May you yield to his cultivation
that is slow, relational, and for your good;
the kind that nurtures something beautiful,
something lasting from within you
and the communion of saints,
across time and space.

May your roots grow deep
where you are planted.
May the land and its history,
the soil of your ancestors,
the climate, and the landscape
of your surroundings
fold you into their story,
shaping a wine unique to your terroir.

May you abide in the True Vine,
drawing from his abundant nourishment
and life that sustains you in all seasons.
May you surrender into his death
and rise with his resurrection power—
bursting with abundance
that springs from his life within.

May you unfold into your truest self
and uncover your belonging
among the branches that shelter and protect you.
May you be generously received
in all your vulnerable beauty,
and receive the gift of others
in a way that transforms you—
cultivating the fruit
that ripens through reciprocity.

The Art of Vinemaking

Together, may you bear the fruit of the kingdom,
the kind that, when harvested and pressed,
yields a wine of enduring quality;
A wine that carries the flavor of Christ,
crushed in the winepress
and poured out as a blessing for the world.

When the cheap wine has run out,
may the world taste its richness and say,
"They've saved the best for last."

Amen.

A Note from the Vinedresser: Dave Bos

"Everything that is in the heavens, on earth, and under the earth is penetrated with connectedness, penetrated with relatedness."[1]

"We shall awaken from our dullness and rise vigorously toward justice. If we fall in love with creation deeper and deeper, we will respond to its endangerment with passion."[2]

That's Hildegard of Bingen speaking similar truths almost a thousand years ago in Germany. She and Bette are kindred spirits when looking at the natural world and the nature of God in it.

When I first met Bette, she was curious about vineyards and working on a piece of art about the vine and vinedresser. It is common for people to want to "check out a vineyard," so of course, I said yes.

When we met, I could tell she was thinking deeply about what I was saying and how I viewed farming and the vine. Most people visit once or a few times and get what they need, but Bette kept coming back ... for years!

She is not done with being in the vineyards and she will continue to dive into vineyards, God's relational world, and how Jesus used the vine to talk about the divine. Her many vintages or seasons in the vineyards have given her a view of depth, beauty, relational wholeness and connection with the vines I have not heard

---

1. Hildegard of Bingen," *Prairiewoods Franciscan Spirituality Center*, accessed July 14, 2025, https://www.healthyhildegard.com/hildegard-bingen-quotes/.

2. Hildegard of Bingen," *Prairiewoods Franciscan Spirituality Center*, accessed July 14, 2025, https://www.healthyhildegard.com/hildegard-bingen-quotes/.

before. Her approach is full of tenacity and grace, which are both needed in the vineyard and in our relationship with Jesus.

She weaves between understanding vineyards and God's Word gracefully. The picture she has painted is of a relational God who is not looking at the bottom line, but who is intentional and hands-on with every pruning cut and every cluster. As a farmer who works with vines (a vinedresser), the perspective of someone coming to this process with new eyes has made me connect even better to vine, vineyard, earth, and God. To think of spiritual flourishing instead of spiritual surviving was life-giving.

A vintage tells a story. A vine tells a longer story. It is never finished, it is alive; we are always growing, producing, fruiting. We always need to be pruned, thinned out, have some fruit drop, struggle and stress in a good way, be harvested, and go dormant. When we stand back and look at the vine, any vine, we can see where it has been and where the vinedresser wants it to go.

Hope is never lost when you understand the multitude of small, intentional decisions from the vinedresser, whether it is to leave fruit behind and focus on growth, or to prune more because last winter was a hard season on the vine.

This is not a one-year view, but a continual renewal in the relationship between the Vinedresser and the Vine. True relationships do not stop, fade, or stay the same. They grow and change. The long view of the vinedresser is always about closer, better, and with more intention. I hope you leave these pages with the spirit of wanting to be closer to, pruned well by, and more focused on, the heart of the Vinedresser.

As I write this, we are at bud break, a most fitting time. I started while the vines were dormant and had the opportunity to write and think during the pruning process. I find myself once again at the start of another amazing vintage—full of struggles, hardships, and challenges, but nevertheless a new chance to grow, understand more fully, and find true connection in this familiar space and rhythmic process.

The rhythmic process of life in a vine is an ancient story and I am grateful Bette is bringing new life and understanding during a time in our culture of such disconnection and discontentment. This is not about perfection in performance, but growing closer to our Creator and his creation, the true source of vitality, and that IT factor we resonate with in the vine and in wine. Taste and see that the Lord is good!

Glossary of Key Terms

Abide: From the Greek word *ménō* (μένω), which means "to remain, dwell, endure, be present, stand, or tarry." According to the *Outline of Biblical Usage* (as found on Blue Letter Bible), it can also mean "not to depart," "to continue to be present," "to be held or kept continually," and "to remain as one, not to become another or different."[1]

Anishinaabek: An Indigenous people native to the Great Lakes region. They include the Ojibwe, Odawa, and Potawatomi peoples.

Attachment: The emotional bonds formed between infants and their caregivers, and the subsequent patterns of behavior this shapes throughout the rest of their lives. These attachments influence a person's ability to cultivate healthy relationships with others.

Biodiversity: The presence of a variety of life forms in an ecosystem; plants, animals, insects, and microorganisms, and their interactions with one another.

Bud Break: The moment in early spring when the first leaves push through the cane branches on the trellis, signaling the start of a new growing season. This usually occurs about a month after pruning.

Cane: A one-year-old branch that has grown from the previous year that is laid down on the trellis during pruning. This is where most of the fruit-bearing shoots will grow out from.

---

1. μένω (menō)," *Blue Letter Bible*, Outline of Biblical Usage by Larry Pierce, accessed July 14, 2025, https://www.blueletterbible.org/lexicon/g3306/niv/mgnt/0-1/.

Cover Crops: Plants used to nourish the soil, increase organic matter, prevent erosion, and support a healthy ecosystem.

Dark Night of the Soul: Often mistaken for depression, the Dark Night of the Soul is a term created by 16th century Spanish mystic St. John of the Cross to describe a time of sensual and spiritual desolation for the purposes of union with God. The journey into and through the Dark Night of the Soul is described in great detail in *The Ascent of Mount Carmel*, and *The Dark Night of the Soul*.

Deciduous: A plant that sheds its leaves annually as they go dormant.

Detachment: The practice of letting go of external attachments that hinder our abiding connection to Christ.

Flourishing Approach: A way of being rooted in the vine through cyclical rhythms of the seasons. Fruitfulness is an overflow of health, quality, and vitality in the vine.

Fruiting Zone: The area of the grapevine near where it is tied to the trellis where the clusters of grapes form and mature.

Grafting: The process of joining two plants so they grow as one. In vines, this involves joining the rootstock (root system) of one grape variety to the shoot of another. It's used to create a new vine with a combination of traits from the rootstock and the adjoined branch.

Head-trained: A vine trained without a trellis, but with branches pruned out from the center to form a crown-like shape.

IFS (Internal Family Systems): "IFS is a transformative tool that conceives of every human being as a system of protective and wounded inner parts led by a core Self. ... IFS is frequently used as an evidence-based psychotherapy, helping people heal by accessing and healing their protective and wounded inner parts. IFS creates inner and outer connectedness by helping people first access their Self and, from that core, come to understand and heal their parts."[2]

Lateral Branches: The smaller, thinner branches that grow horizontally from the shoots that grow vertically from the cane (branch on the trellis).

Microbial Life: The unseen, diverse array of microorganisms, including: bacteria, algae, protozoa, fungi, and archaea.

Monocropping: The practice of planting a single crop repeatedly to maximize output.

Productivity-Driven Approach: A mindset that prioritizes output, achievement, and measurable results over inner transformation and growth.

Pruning: The process of intentionally cutting back a vine to manage growth, improve fruit quality, and maintain a vine's health. Vines are pruned to direct energy where a vinedresser wants it to go, toward growth, healing, and/or fruit.

Rootstock: The root system onto which a vine is grafted. It provides disease resistance and support to the new branch.

Rule of Life: A Rule of Life is an ancient practice that people of faith have used to order and orient their lives individually and in community. The purpose is to help one another draw nearer to the Way of Jesus through set rhythms, intentions and actions. Examples include St. Benedict's Rule, The Rule of the Friars Minor, The Rule of St. Basil, and The Rule of Life for the Poor Clares. Protestant and even secular organizations now recommend Rules of Life for the modern context.

---

2. Internal Family Systems Institute, "What Is IFS?," *IFS Institute*, accessed June 19, 2025, https://ifs-institute.com/.

Tendrils: The slender, curling tips of branches that help the vine climb upward during the growing season.

Terroir: The way a wine uniquely reflects the context where a vine grows from year to year. The Four Primary Influences on Terroir: soil, climate, landscape, and tradition (the particular cultivation practices of a vinedresser often passed down from generation to generation, such as pruning techniques, canopy management, and harvest timing).

True Self/False Self: These are psychological and spiritual descriptions of the tension of identity most people experience. The True Self is the YOU that most fully reflects the image of God within you. It is your deepest, truest, most coherent and authentic identity. This stands in contrast to the False Self, which stems from those parts of us that react with fear, shame, anger, pain, and guilt in an effort to protect ourselves. Thomas Merton argues that the only way back into the true self—and back into union with God, for which we were made—is to journey back through the heart of the false self, to see it for what it is in all its illusion and delusion, and to come out the other side into the light of God's truth.[3]

Vinedresser: A farmer who cultivates vines.

Vintner: A person who oversees the winemaking process from vine to bottle.

Vitality: The life-force or inner energy of the vine.

Suckering: The process of removing unwanted growth from the base or lower trunk of the vine. These shoots do not contribute to fruit production.

---

3 James Finley, *Merton's Palace of Nowhere* (Notre Dame, IN: Ave Maria Press, 1978).

Trellis: A supportive structure that holds up the vine. The main cane branch is tied down to the trellis after pruning and will support its growth through the growing season.

Acknowledgements

They say it takes a village to raise a child—and in many ways, it takes a village to bring a book to life. I am profoundly grateful to the community that made *The Art of Vinemaking* possible.

Dave Bos, thank you for investing so deeply—your time, wisdom, and friendship opened my eyes to the vineyard and to the heart of God. You've been a living picture of the Vinedresser.

Jackie Bos, thank you for modeling beauty, hospitality, and intentionality. Your insights and the table you and Dave set—both literally and spiritually—shaped this work.

Bethany Blankespoor, from vineyard treks to soul-deep conversations, thank you for walking closely with me in this journey and embodying what it means to abide.

Aaron White, I am deeply grateful for your friendship and companionship along this journey. Your gifts in project management and editing, combined with your encouragement, brought clarity and confidence at every stage of the process.

Thank you to those who partnered with **Boundless Publishing** to bring this book to life: Jude May, Allison Mangrum, Vicki Frye, Joel Varner, and Krissie Kramer—for your creative work in design, editing, typesetting, and marketing.

Kara Yuza, thank you for your faithful partnership behind the scenes. Your tireless work allowed me to focus on what only I could do.

Danielle Strickland, your surrendered, joy-filled life has called me forth. Thank you for creating Boundless, for loving me so specifically, and for always making me laugh.

Ang Lam, your mentorship has redefined leadership for me. Thank you for your wisdom, empathy, and truth-telling at critical moments.

Timo and Siobhan Koch, thank you for your friendship and support throughout this creative process.

Brenda Renderos, Lila Weber, and Alicia Wilson, thank you for your honest feedback and perspective as women of color—your words helped me see more clearly.

To my Boundless Family, thank you for welcoming every part of me and modeling love in action. I'm honored to belong to you.

The Vine Club—especially Elizabeth, Jo, Janae, Deb, Natalie, Katharine, Peggy, Karen, Jennifer, Hannah, Brent, Catherine, Camie, Barb, Jim, Erica, Cheryl, Ruth—thank you for your belief, feedback, and generous encouragement in the early stages.

Awakening the Soul Board Members, thank you for stewarding this vision with prayerful wisdom, spiritual grounding, and steady support.

Ministry Partners and Investors, thank you for crowd-funding this dream into reality. Your trust carried it forward.

Prayer Team, thank you for holding me and this book in prayer at every step.

Susie Lipps, thank you for diving in with such joy, wisdom, and love for the vine.

Curt Thompson, MD, thank you for how your teaching and friendship have liberated and empowered me as an artist.

Julie Quinn, thank you for your generous hospitality and belief in me as I created.

Acknowledgements

Sharon Brown, thank you for holding space for me—and for the Spirit—since seminary.

Troy and Faith Bierma at The Hermitage, thank you for cultivating a sacred space that shaped both this book and my soul.

Deb Griest, thank you for walking closely with me, both as a spiritual director and as a friend who believed in this from the beginning.

Kristen Selle, thank you for your partnership and for modeling a life rooted in creation's wisdom and partnering in setting the table for our retreat.

Mom and Dad Dickinson, thank you for supporting our family while I wrote.

Mom, Dad, Jess, and Mel, thank you for helping shape me into who I am—and always cheering me on.

Isaiah and Winston, thank you for the trampoline dances, cuddles, and joy that kept me going.

Steven, thank you for investing in this work with your whole self— through feedback, support, and love. You believed in the work "in my gut," and I couldn't have done this without you.

To my endorsers, thank you for lending your words to this message and helping it reach others with hope and beauty.

And Jesus, the True Vine—thank You for being my source, sustainer, and friend. Thank you for re-anchoring me of my Belovedness throughout the process. Everything good in this book has come from You.

About the Author

Bette Dickinson is a prophetic artist, writer, and speaker who invites audiences to connect with God through visual parables of the spiritual journey. In 2021, she founded *Awakening the Soul*, a ministry that creates resources and experiences to awaken the souls of ministry leaders through beauty and wonder.

Bette's work integrates art, Scripture, and spiritual practices to cultivate spaces of encounter with God. She has partnered with organizations such as Barna, World Vision, InterVarsity, Infinitum, and churches all over the world to guide leaders and communities into deeper spiritual formation through the lens of beauty.

She holds a Master of Divinity in Pastoral Studies from Grand Rapids Theological Seminary and is the author of *Making Room in Advent: 25 Devotions for a Season of Wonder* (InterVarsity Press, 2022), a visual and devotional journey through the season of Advent.

Bette lives in Traverse City, Michigan, with her husband and their two boys.

Learn more at www.bettedickinson.com

The Art of Vinemaking Journey

Go Deeper: Join the Art of Vinemaking Journey

The Art of Vinemaking is not just a book—it's a movement of spiritual formation rooted in the rhythms of creation. If your soul longs for a slower, sacred rhythm of abiding, we'd love for you to continue the journey with us.

Explore These Ways to Go Deeper:

Online Courses
4 online courses aligned with the content from the book and designed to integrate spiritual practices and lessons from the vine into your daily life. Includes:
- Exclusive interviews with author Bette Dickinson and organic vinedresser Dave Bos
- Introductory videos, creative spiritual practices, and reflection questions
- Guided audio and video resources (including audio-guided walks and visio divina videos)

Guided Cohorts
Engage in rich conversation and communal transformation as you process the material with others on the same path.

Vineyard Retreats
Step away from the noise and immerse yourself in the beauty of the vineyard. These retreats offer space to slow down, listen deeply, and be tended by the Vinedresser.

Whether you find yourself in a season of life, death, or resurrection, these experiences will help you embody a way of life that bears lasting fruit.

Custom Experiences for Teams & Groups
Looking for something designed specifically for your ministry, church, or leadership team? Bette offers customized retreats and experiences tailored to your community's unique needs.

Learn more and join the movement at:
www.theartofvinemaking.com

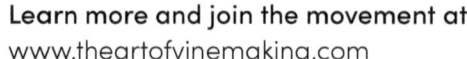